The Alphabet
Learning Its Letters and Sounds

Grades PreSchool to Kindergarten

Written by Ruth Solski
Illustrated by Kevin Jackson

About the author:

Ruth Solski was an educator for 30 years. She has written many educational resources and is the founder of S&S Learning Materials. As a writer, her main goal is to provide teachers with a useful tool that they can implement in their classrooms to bring the joy of learning to students.

ISBN 978-1-55495-038-6
Copyright 2010

Published in the U.S.A by:
On The Mark Press
P.O. Box 433
Clayton, New York
13624
www.onthemarkpress.com

Published in Canada by:
S&S Learning Materials
15 Dairy Avenue
Napanee, Ontario
K7R 1M4
www.sslearning.com

At A Glance

Learning Expectations	Letter Recognition	Sound Recognition of	Review Activities
Understanding concepts			
Identify upper case letters	•		
Identify lower case letters	•		
Identify concept of an alphabet	•		
Applying Motor Skills			
Tracing letter forms	•	•	•
Using left to right progression	•	•	•
Coloring within limits	•	•	•
Following oral direction	•	•	•
Visual Discrimination			
Naming upper and lower case letters	•	•	•
Recognizing likes and differences in letters	•	•	•
Understanding letter formation	•	•	•
Applying visual discrimination skills	•	•	•
Auditory Skills			
Recognize letter sounds		•	
Follows oral directions	•	•	•

Table Of Contents

The Alphabet

Learning Its Letters and Sounds

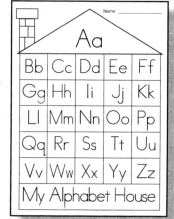

About this Book:

This resource has been designed to teach students the names and formations of the twenty-six upper and lower case letters of the alphabet. The introduction of the letters' sounds is to be done informally to develop student awareness.

Contents of the Resource:

- Reproducible Cover for an Alphabet book
- Twenty-Six Lessons and Follow-up Activities to Develop the Recognition and Formation of the Letters
- Twenty-Six Lessons and Follow-Up Activities to Review Letters' Names and Formations and to Introduce Letter Sounds
- Fourteen Reproducible Visual Discrimination Activities
- Twenty-Six Review Letter Activities

Materials Required for Individual Letter Lessons:

- Letters of the alphabet should be displayed in the classroom at a level the students can view and use easily.
- Locate letters of the alphabet that students can use to trace, feel, and play with at a center. There are many types available today that can be used to develop tactile abilities such as letters made out of sandpaper, cardboard, paper, plastic, felt, and those that are magnetic.
- Locate large alphabet cards that have only the letters to use for the teaching of formations and directions of lines and shapes.
- Look for poems and poetry books on the alphabet. Use the poems during the various lessons.
- Locate different types of alphabet books and share them with your students. Place them around the classroom.
- Make up alphabet stories and riddles for your students.
- Sing different alphabet songs.

Teaching Organization:

Each letter of the alphabet has two lessons. The first lesson is designed to introduce the letter and its formation. The second lesson is designed to review the letter's name and its formation and to introduce the sound or sounds it makes.

Each student should be provided with a scrapbook that has at least 30 pages to be used as an individual alphabet book and will hold 8 ½" by 11" sheets comfortably. The reproducible cover for the alphabet book found on page 7, should be glued to the scrapbook's cover.

As the students learn new letters of the alphabet, the room in which the letter lives in the alphabet house is to be colored.

Each page that bears an upper and lower case letter and a picture should be glued in the alphabet scrapbook after the lesson and after the students have colored it. The review page is not to be glued into the alphabet scrapbook and may be taken home or placed in a student file folder.

Review Lessons:

Letter names and formations should be continually reviewed. Use the pages found on pages 112 to 118 to review upper and lower case letters and to develop visual discrimination.

These pages have been designed so they may be cut in half to form two small worksheets and used when needed. Use the pages found on 119 to 144 to review individual letters taught. The students will identify upper and lower case letters and trace lines to form letters.

Sound Strategies:

Young students recall letter and sound recognition quicker using an auditory and verbal strategy that can be turned into a game-like situation. These devices have been used in the classroom and have achieved great success.

1. Hold up or point to a letter in the alphabet. Have the students say its name and its sound.

2. The teacher makes the sound. Student names and locates the letter in the alphabet.

3. Give the students a clue, e.g., It makes the sound of a machine gun. What is the letter's name. Show us where it is in the alphabet.

4. Students can give the clues and ask other students to locate the letter in the alphabet.

Aa: Short a - looking in the mouth sound when you go to the doctor - aah, aah
     Long a - says its own name

Bb: buh-buh-buh - babbling brook sound heard in the spring

Cc: cuh-cuh-cuh - coughing sound

Dd: duh-duh-duh - machine gun sound when it is firing

Ee: Long e - say its own name or scared sound
     Short e - so what sound - eh

Ff: f-f-f - angry cat sound

Gg: guh-guh-guh - monkey gargling his throat because it is sore sound

Hh: huh-huh-huh - out of breath sound

Ii: Long i - says it own name
     Short i - don't know sound - ih

Jj: juh-juh-juh - teeth chattering sound

Kk: kih-kih-kih - coughing sound

Ll: ul-ul-ul - licking the lollipop sound

Mm: m-m-m - tasting good sound

Nn: n-n-n - the nose tickling sound

Oo: Long o - says its own name or the surprised sound
     Short o - disappointed sound "aw"

Pp: puh-puh-puh - popcorn popping in the pan sound

Qq: quh-quh-quh - duck sound

Rr: r-r-r - dog growling sound

Ss: s-s-s - Sammy Snake hissing sound

Tt: tih-tih-tih - clock ticking sound

Uu: Long u - says its own name
      Short u - didn't hear you sound - uh

Vv: vih-vih-vih - bottom lip buzzing sound or bottom lip tickling sound

Ww: wuh-wuh-wuh - windy sound

Xx: ks-s-s - kissing sound

Yy: yuh-yuh-yuh - bad way of saying yes sound

Zz: z-z-z - - buzzing sound

Name: _____

Aa

Bb	Cc	Dd	Ee	Ff
Gg	Hh	Ii	Jj	Kk
Ll	Mm	Nn	Oo	Pp
Qq	Rr	Ss	Tt	Uu
Vv	Ww	Xx	Yy	Zz

My Alphabet House

OTM-18103 • SSR1-103 The Alphabet

Teaching the Recognition of the Letter "Aa"

Objectives:

- To reinforce the recognition of the upper and lower case forms of the letter "Aa."
- To develop an awareness of letter formation and how they are made.

Introduction:

Use a large alphabet card and letter "Aa" cutouts. Pass the letters out to your students allowing them to trace around the shape of the letters with their fingers. Discuss the types of lines in each letter, noting straight lines, round lines, and the number of lines.

Discussion:

1. Does anyone know the name of this letter? Where does this letter live? (Point to the alphabet.) It lives with 25 other letters in a big house called the alphabet. Does anyone have this letter in their name? Explain to the students that the letter "Aa" has two shapes; a big shape and a little shape.

2. Talk about the shape of the upper case "A." Draw your students' attention to its straight lines that come to a point like a mountain with a road going from one side to the other. Trace its shape with your finger. Begin at the top and go down the left side. Lift your finger and go to the top of the letter "A" and go down the right side. Then go to the left side to follow the road that connects both sides and move your finger to the right.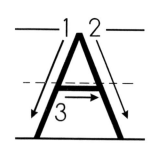

3. Have the students do the same movements on letters that they have; in the air; on a table; on the palm of their hand using their fingers.

4. Discuss the shape of the lower case "a." Trace the "a" to show its formation. Explain that the small "a" is made of a ball and a stick. The stick is pushing the ball ahead of it. Practice tracing the small "a" using the methods used for the upper case "A." Begin at the top of the ball and trace all the way around it moving from the left to the right. Then trace the stick from the top to the bottom so that it kisses the ball. Practice these movements frequently to remind students of the correct ways to form the letters. These movements will be used during the written form on paper and will reinforce left to right progression used in reading and writing.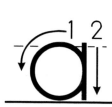

Student Activity: Alphabet Book

1. Reproduce page 9 with the letter "Aa" for your students.

2. Discuss the shapes of the letters. Encourage your students to color the letters in the same directions in which they traced them neatly.

3. Instruct your students to neatly color the ape. What is an ape? Where might one live? What do apes like to eat?

4. Discuss the words that say ape at the bottom of the sheet. Have the students identify the word with the upper case "A" and the word with the lower case "a."

5. Glue this page into a scrapbook to make a student alphabet book.

6. Glue the reproducible cover found on page 7 on the front of the scrapbook. Have the students color the part of the house that the letter Aa lives in. Explain that the letter "Aa" lives in the attic.

7. Recite this rhyme with your students.

> A is for Amy the Ape,
> Who flies in the sky.
> Wearing a red cape,
> As she passes by.

Ape ape

Teaching the Recognition of the Letter "Aa" and Its Sounds

Objectives:

- To reinforce the recognition of the letter "Aa" and to introduce the sounds that it makes.
- To strengthen listening skills and the ability to follow directions.
- To develop and improve communication skills.

Reproduce page 11 for your students.

Teacher Directed Activity:

1. Look at the letters at the top of the page. What are their names? (Aa)

2. Let's make them in the air, on the paper, etc. with your fingers. Remind them where to start and stop and the direction of flow.

3. Let's look at the pictures on the page. Point to each one as I say its name.

   acorn,   ant,   alligator,   apron

4. Use your green crayon and color the "acorn." While the children are coloring, discuss the picture. What is an acorn? Where does it grow? Who might eat an acorn? What other things grow on trees?

5. Listen to the beginning of "acorn." Exaggerate the long "a" sound at the start of the word so the students can hear it. Have them echo you. Tell them the "Aa" is talking. What is it saying? (It is saying its own name.)

6. Point to the picture of the "ant." Neatly color the ant with your black crayon. Discuss the picture. What is an ant? Where does an ant live? Where do you see ants? Can you think of the names of other insects?

7. Listen to the beginning of "ant." Exaggerate the sound the "a" makes. Have the students repeat the word. Have them place their hands under their jaws and say "ant." They will notice that their jaws drop and their mouths are open wide.

8. Find the "alligator." Put a big red dot on it. Color the alligator any color you like. Discuss the picture. Where does an alligator live? What does it like to eat? Can you think of other animals that live in the water?

9. Listen while I say the word "alligator." Exaggerate the "a" sound. The letter "Aa" is talking at the beginning of alligator. Put your hand under your chin. Say alligator. Can you hear it? What does it say? (ah) What does your chin do? (It drops.)

10. Put your finger on the "apron." Color it blue. Discuss the picture. What is an apron? What is it used for? Who in your house might wear one?

11. Listen while I say the word "apron." Exaggerate the "Aa" sound. The letter "Aa" is talking at the beginning of apron. Can you hear it? What does it say? (Its own name.) Say "apron."

12. Listen while I say the names of the pictures. Say each word in an exaggerated fashion at the beginning. Have the children say them with you. Do all the pictures sound the same at the beginning when I say them? (No) Can you tell which pictures begin the same way?

13. Have the students repeat what you say. a) ant, apron (No)   b) ant, alligator (Yes)
    c) apron, acorn (Yes)   d) ant, acorn (No)

14. Explain to the students that the letter "Aa" can make two sounds. It can say its own name or its other sound "ah". Reinforce that the "long a" sound makes you open your mouth a little while the "short a" sound makes your jaw drop and your mouth to open wide.

Conclusions: Sing the alphabet song.

A a

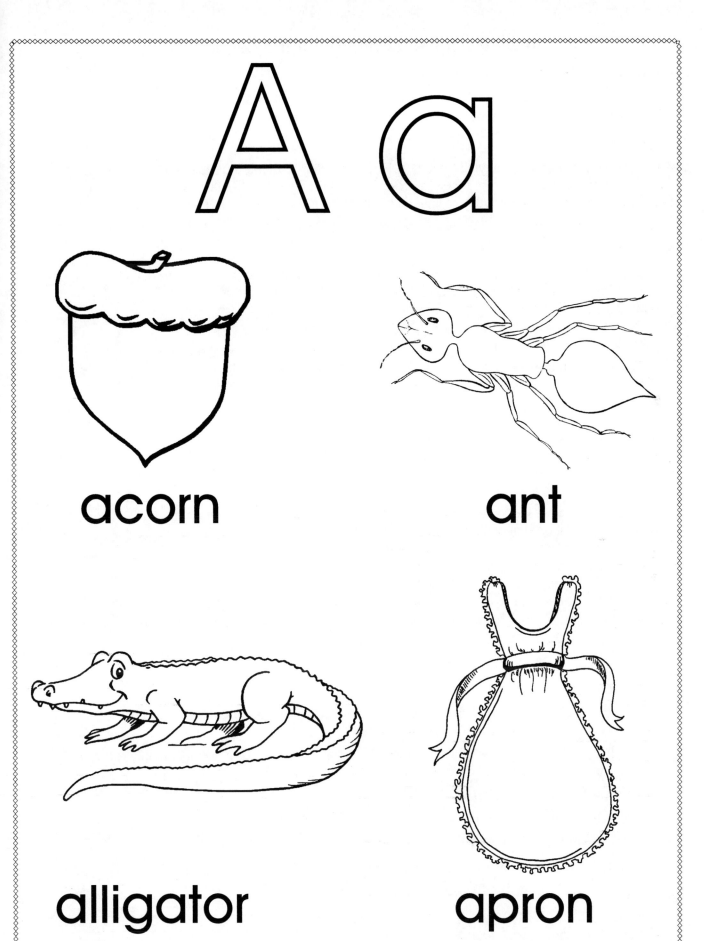

acorn

ant

alligator

apron

Teaching the Recognition of the Letter "Bb"

Objectives:
- To reinforce the recognition of the upper and lower case forms of the letter "Bb."
- To develop an awareness of the letter formation and how it is made.

Introduction:
Use a large alphabet card displaying the letter "Bb" and letter "Bb" cutouts. Pass the letters out to your students allowing them to trace around the letters with their fingers to note their shapes. Discuss the types of lines in each letter. Note the straight lines, the curved or rounded lines, the number of lines, and the direction that the letters are walking or facing.

Discussion:
1. Does anyone know the name of this letter? It is called the letter "Bb." Where does this letter live in the alphabet. (Point to the alphabet.) It lives in a room beside the letter "Aa" and is the second letter in the alphabet. Does anyone have this letter in their name? Print their names on the chalkboard and have the students circle the letter "Bb" in each one.

2. Talk about the shape of the upper case "B" and the lower case "b." The big "B" has a straight back with a face and a big fat tummy. Make the upper case "B" on chart paper and in the air with your finger. Always work from top to bottom and from left to right. Show its back with a motion going from the top to the bottom. Then make the rounded face moving from left to right making a curved line. Next make the big fat tummy going from left to right. Emphasize that when you make the "B" there are 3 definite movements. Have the students mimic your movements in the air, on a table, on the floor, and on the palm of their hand using their fingers.

3. Discuss the shape of the lower case "b." Trace the "b" or print it on chart paper to show its formation. The little "b" has a tall stick that pushes a ball. Make the motion in the air. Always start at the top of the straight line and go down to the bottom. Make the motion in the air. Do the same while making the ball reinforcing left to right progression. Tell the students the ball must kiss the stick. Practice these movements frequently to remind students of the correct ways to form the letters. This practice will help children to print letters properly on lines.

Student Activity: Alphabet Book
1. Reproduce page 13 with the letter "Bb" for your students.

2. Discuss the letter shapes. Encourage your students to color the letters in the same directions in which they traced them with their fingers in the air.

3. Discuss the bear and its name at the bottom of the page. Have your students identify the word with the upper case "B" and the word with the lower case "b."

4. Glue this page into each student's alphabet scrapbook.

5. Have the students color the room in the alphabet house where the "Bb" lives.

6. Teach this rhyme about the letter "Bb" to your students. Have them recite it with you.

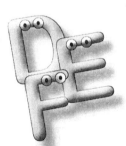

> "Bb" is for big bear,
> Hunting near some trees.
> Looking for sweet honey,
> Made by busy bees.

7. Review letters, formations, sounds, and rhymes previously learned.

Bear   bear

Teaching the Recognition of the Letter "Bb" and Its Sound

Objectives:

- To reinforce the recognition of the letter "Bb" and to introduce the sound that it makes.
- To strengthen listening skills and the ability to follow directions.
- To develop and improve communication skills.

Reproduce page 15 for your students.

Teacher Directed Activity:

1. Look at the letters at the top of the page. What are they called? (Bb)

2. Let's trace them with our fingers. Let's make them in the air. Constantly reinforce starting positions and the direction in which each part flows.

3. Let's look at the pictures on the page. Point to each one and say its name.

   butterfly,   bee,   bell,   boat

4. Using your crayons neatly color the butterfly. While the children are working discuss the picture. Have you ever seen a real butterfly? Where might you see one? How does a butterfly move about? What does it use to fly? A butterfly is an insect. Can you think of the names of other insects?

5. Color the bee yellow. Where would you see a bee? Where does a bee live? What do bees make? What does a bee sometimes do to people? What sound does a bee make? (buzz) Does its sound begin the same way as its name? Say the word "bee." Now say the word "buzz." Now say "Bees buzz." Do they begin with the same sound? (Yes)

6. Color the bell orange. Where might you see a bell? What sound does a big bell make? (bong, bong) Say the words "Big bell bongs." Do they all begin the same way? (Yes)

7. Color the boat brown. Where might you see a boat? What can you do on a boat? Have you ever been in a boat? Can you think of a kind of boat?

8. Point to each picture and say its name.

   butterfly,   bee,   bell,   boat

   What sound do you hear at the beginning of each picture? (buh) When you make the sound at the beginning of butterfly, bee, bell and boat where are your lips? (They are pressed together.) I call this the babbling brook sound. When a stream has lots of water it makes a buh-buh-buh sound as it flows.

Auditory Game:

- Listen while I say two words: **boy, bed**
- Do they begin the same way? (Yes) What sound do you hear? (buh)
- Listen again. Clap your hands if the words begin with "Bb" (buh).
- Say each pair of words clearly and slowly. Exaggerate the initial sounds.

  a) bone, apple (No Response)   b) bicycle, barn (Response)   c) acorn, button (No Response)
  d) band, big (Response)   e) alligator, box (No Response)   f) bugle, bumper (Response)
  g) boots, house (No Response)   h) bone, bark (Response)   i) banana, apple (No Response)

Conclusions:

- Sing the alphabet song.
- Review the letters, formations, sounds, and rhymes previously taught.

B b

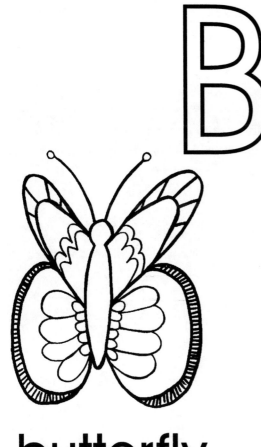

butterfly

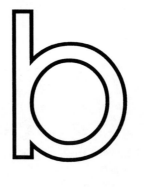

bee

bell

boat

OTM-18103 • SSR1-103 The Alphabet

Teaching the Recognition of the Letter "Cc"

Objectives:

- To reinforce the recognition of the upper and lower case forms of the letter "Cc."
- To develop an awareness of its letter formation.

Introduction:

Use a large alphabet card and letter "Cc" cutouts. Pass the letters out to your students allowing them to trace each letter with their fingers to note their shapes. Discuss the type of lines used in the letter such as curved or rounded.

Discussion:

1. Does anyone know the name of this letter? (Cc) Explain to your students the letter "Cc" is shaped like a cookie with a bite out of it. Where does the letter "Cc" live? (Point to the alphabet.) It lives in the room next to the letter "Bb."

2. Discuss the shape of the letter. Explain where it starts and where it ends. Have the students note that both letters look the same and tell them they are made the same way. One "C" is bigger than the other "c." Have the students trace the letter "Cc" with their fingers in the air, on the table, the floor, and the palm of their hands. Make sure that they start at the top and move toward the left leaving a hole in it. Practice these movements frequently.

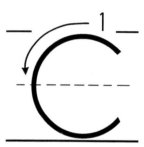

Student Activity: Alphabet Book

1. Reproduce page 17 with the letter "Cc" for your students.

2. Discuss the shape of the letters. Encourage your students to color the letters in the same direction in which they traced each one neatly.

3. Have them color the cat.

4. Discuss the words that say "cat" at the bottom of the page. Have them identify the word "Cat" that has the big "C" and then have them identify the word "cat" with the little "c."

5. Glue this page into their alphabet scrapbook.

6. Have the students color the room in the **Alphabet House** where the letter "Cc" lives.

7. Recite this rhyme with the students. Have them say it with you.

> "Cc" is for cat,
> Who sleeps everywhere.
> On the kitchen mat,
> And on a big chair.

8. Review the letters, formations, sounds, and rhymes previously learned.

Cc Cat cat

 OTM-18103 • SSR1-103 The Alphabet

Teaching the Recognition of the Letter "Cc" and Its Sound

Objectives:

- To reinforce the recognition of the letter "Cc" and to introduce the sound that it makes.
- To strengthen listening skills and the ability to follow directions.
- To develop and improve communication skills.

Reproduce page 19 for your students.

Teacher Directed Activity:

1. Look at the two letters at the top of the page. What are they called? (Cc)

2. Let's trace them with our fingers on the paper. Let's make them in the air. Constantly reinforce starting positions and the direction in which each part of the letter flows.

3. Let's look at the pictures on this page. Point to each one while I say their names.

   camel,   candle,   castle,   candy cane

4. Using your brown crayon, neatly color the camel. While the children are working, discuss the picture. What is a camel? Where does a camel live? What does he have on his back? How do people use camels? The camel is an animal. Can you think of the names of other animals?

5. Put your finger on the candle. Now neatly color the candle purple. What is a candle? What is a candle used for? How do people use candles? What are candles made of? Why are candles dangerous?

6. Put your finger on the castle. Color the castle green. What is a castle? Who may live in a castle? In what kind of stories are castles found?

7. Put your finger on the candy cane. Color the candy cane red and white. When do we see candy canes? Have you ever eaten one? How does a candy cane taste? Where are they hung sometimes?

8. Point to each picture as I say its name. Exaggerate the initial sound as you say each word.

   camel,   candle,   castle,   candy cane

   What sound do you hear at the beginning of each word? (cuh) The letter "Cc" makes the coughing sound. Demonstrate the sound. Have the students mimic the coughing sound. When you make this sound where does it come from? (back of my throat or mouth)

Auditory Game:

- Listen while I say two words: **coffee, cactus**
- Do they begin the same way? (Yes) What sound do you hear at the beginning? (cuh)
- This time clap your hands if the words begin with "Cc," the coughing sound.
- Say the following groups of words and wait for a reponse.

   a) car, zoo (No Response)   b) cook, burn (No Response)   c) cookie, cake (Response)
   d) candy, coin (Response)   e) monkey, can (No Response)   f) cup, candle (Response)
   g) caterpiller, carpet (Response)   h) corn, pocket (No Response)   i) cow, corner (Response)

Conclusion:

- Sing the alphabet song.
- Review the letters, formations, sounds, and rhymes previously taught.

C c

camel

candle

castle

candy cane

Teaching the Recognition of the Letter "Dd"

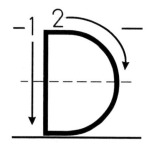

Objectives:

- To reinforce the recognition of the upper and lower case forms of the letter "Dd."
- To develop an awareness of the letter formation and how it is made.

Introduction:

Use a large alphabet card and letter "Dd" cutouts. Pass the letters out to your students. Allow them to trace around the letters with their fingers to note their shapes. Discuss the types of lines in each letter noting straight lines, round lines, curved lines, and the number of lines.

Discussion:

1. Does anyone know the name for these letters. (Hold up the upper case "D" and the lower case "d.") Where do they live (Point to the alphabet.) They live in a big house called the alphabet. In which room do they live? (They live in the room beside the letter "Cc.") Does anyone have these letters in their name? Who has the big "D?" Who has the little "d?"

2. Explain to the students that the letters called "Dd" have two shapes, a big shape and a little shape. Talk about the shape of the upper case "D." Draw their attention to its straight back and its big fat tummy. Trace its shape with your finger. Begin at the top of the straight line and go down to the bottom. Proceed to the top again and then trace the curved line moving from the left to the right and then back to the left. Have your students complete the same movements on the letters that they have, in the air, on a table, and on the palm of their hands using their fingers.

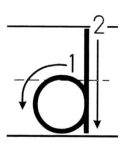

3. Discuss the shape of the lower case "d." Trace the "d" to show its formation Explain that the small "d" is made of a ball and a stick. The ball is being followed by a stick that is pushing it. Practice tracing the small "d" using the same methods for the upper case "D." Begin at the top of the ball and trace all the way around the ball from the left to the right. Then start at the top of the straight line and move down to the bottom. Tell the students in the letter "d" the stick kisses the ball on the right side.

Student Activity: Alphabet Book

1. Reproduce page 21 with the letter "Dd" for your students.

2. Discuss the shapes of the letters. Encourage your students to color the letters neatly in the same directions in which they traced them.

3. Have them neatly color the dog.

4. Discuss the words that say "dog." Have the students identify the word with the big "D" and then have them identify the word with the little "d."

5. Glue this page into the students' alphabet scrapbook.

6. Have the students color the room in which the letter "Dd" lives on the **Alphabet House** page.

7. Recite this rhyme with the students.

> "Dd" is for dog,
> Who barks to say.
> It's time for me,
> To go out and play.

8. Review the letters, formations, sounds, and rhymes previously taught.

Dog dog

 OTM-18103 • SSR1-103 The Alphabet

Teaching the Recognition of the Letter "Dd" and Its Sound

Objectives:

- To reinforce the recognition of the letter "Dd" and to introduce the sound that it makes.
- To strengthen listening skills and the ability to follow directions.
- To develop and improve communication skills.

Reproduce page 23 for your students.

Teacher Directed Activity:

1. Look at the letters at the top of the page. What are their names? (Dd)

2. Let's trace each one with our fingers. Let's make each one in the air. Constantly reinforce starting positions and the direction in which each part of the letter flows.

3. Let's look at the pictures on the page. Point to each one, while I say their names.

   deer,   dinosaur,   duck,   dish

4. Using your crayons, neatly color the deer brown. While the students are working, discuss the picture. Have you ever seen a real deer? Where might you see one? What do you think a deer eats? What can a deer do if a fence is in its way? Can you think of other animals that live in the woods?

5. Put your finger on the dinosaur. Color it green. Can you see dinosaurs today? When did they live? How big were dinosaurs? Do you know the names of any dinosaurs?

6. Put your finger on the duck. Color it yellow. Where might you find a duck? What sound does a duck make? What covers the outside of a duck? What do ducks eat? What can ducks do well?

7. Find the dish and color it blue. What is a dish used for? Where do you put a dish when you want to use it? Where do you put a dish when it is dirty? Where do you put a dish when it is clean? What happens sometimes when you drop a dish?

8. Point to each picture and listen while I say its name. Exaggerate the beginning sound as you say each word.

   deer,   dinosaur,   duck,   dish

What sound do you hear at the beginning of each picture? (duh) Have the students say the names of the pictures. When you say the sound at the beginning of deer, dinosaur, duck, and dish are your lips together? (No) Where is your tongue? (Pressing on the roof of my mouth above my front teeth.) I call this sound the machine gun sound because, when a machine gun is fired it goes duh-duh-duh-duh-duh. Have the students practice saying the sound. This is one way students can differentiate between the sounds that "Bb" and "Pp" make.

Auditory Game:

- Listen while I say two words: **doll, door**
- Do they begin the same way? (Yes) What sound do you hear? (duh)
- Listen again. This time, clap your hands if the words begin with "Dd."
- Say the following groups of words and wait for a response.

   a) donut, door (Response)   b) barn, dart (No Response)   c) dolphin, desk (Response)
   d) pig, doll (No Response)   e) dice, dig (Response)   f) bell, deep (No Response)
   g) dollar, dishes (Response)   h) box, dinosaur (No Response)   i) bowl, bear (Response)

Conclusion:

- Sing the alphabet song.
- Review the letters, formations, sounds, and rhymes that have been previously taught.

D d

deer

dinosaur

duck

dish

Teaching the Recognition of the Letter "Ee"

Objectives:

- To reinforce the recognition of the upper and lower case forms of the letter "Ee."
- To develop an awareness of the letter formation and how it is made.

Introduction:

Use a large alphabet card and letter "Ee" cutouts. Pass the letters out to your students. Allow them to trace around the shape of the letters with their fingers to note their shapes and lines. Discuss the types of lines in each letter noting straight lines, where they intersect, round or curved lines, and the number of lines.

Discussion:

1. Does anyone know the name for these letters? (Hold up the upper case "E" and the lower case "e.") Where do these letters live? (Point to the alphabet.) They live with 25 other letters in a big house called the alphabet. In which room do they live? (They live in the room beside the letter Dd.) Does anyone have this letter in their name. (Hold up the big "E.") Who has the little "e"? (Hold up the little "e.")

2. Explain to the students that the letters called "Ee" have two shapes, a big shape and a little shape. Talk about the shape of the upper case "E." (Hold up the letter.) Draw the students' attention to its straight back and three arms. Two arms are long and one arm is little. Trace its shape with your finger. Begin at the top of the vertical line and then travel down it to the bottom. Next trace each horizontal line from left to right. Have your students complete the same movements on the letters that they have as well as in the air, on a table, and on the palm of their hands using their fingers.

3. Discuss the shape of the lower case "e." Trace the "e" to show its formation. Explain that the small "e" is made of a straight line and a curved line that is almost like a circle. Practice tracing the small "e" using the same methods used for the upper case "E." Begin by making a horizontal line that goes from left to right. Then start at the right end of the line to make a curved line similar to a small "c."

Student Activity: Alphabet Book

1. Reproduce page 25 with the letter "Ee" for your students.

2. Discuss the shapes of the letters. Encourage your students to color the letters in the same directions in which they traced them neatly.

3. Have them neatly color the eagle.

4. Discuss the words at the bottom of the page that say "eagle." Have the students identify the word with the big "E" and then have them identify the word that begins with the little "e." Draw to their attention that there is a small "e" at the end of each word.

5. Glue this page into the students' alphabet scrapbook.

6. Have the students color the room in which the letter "Ee" lives on the Alphabet House page.

7. Recite this rhyme with the students.

> "Ee" is for eagle,
> Flapping big wings.
> Flies up high,
> Like a big bird king.

8. Review the letters, formations, sounds, and rhymes of letters previously taught.

Eagle eagle

OTM-18103 • SSR1-103 The Alphabet

Teaching the Recognition of the Letter "Ee" and Its Sounds

Objectives:

- To reinforce the recognition of the letter "Ee" and to introduce the sounds that it makes.
- To strengthen listening skills and the ability to follow directions.
- To develop and improve communication skills.

Reproduce page 27 for your students.

Teacher Directed Activity:

1. Look at the letters at the top of the page. What are their names? (Ee)

2. Let's trace each one with our fingers. Let's make one in the air. Constantly reinforce starting positions and the direction in which each part flows and stops.

3. Let's look at the pictures on the page. Point to each one while I say its name.

   ears,   elf,   egg,   Easter Bunny

4. Use your yellow crayon to color the ear. While the students are working, discuss the picture. What are ears? Who has ears? Where are your ears? How many ears do you have? What do you use your ears for? Listen to the beginning of the word "ears." Exaggerate the long "e" sound at the beginning of the word, so the children can hear it. Have them echo you. Tell them the "Ee" is talking? What is it saying? Have the students make the sound. (It is saying its own name.)

5. Find the picture of an egg. Put blue dots on it. Discuss the picture. Have you ever seen an egg? What shape is an egg? What do we call the outside of an egg? Which part do we eat? Where do eggs come from? Listen while I say the word egg. Exaggerate the short "e" sound. The letter "Ee" is talking at the beginning of egg. Put your hand on your throat again and make the sound "eh" and feel the vibration.

6. Point to the picture of the elf. Neatly color the elf green. Discuss the picture. What is an elf? Where might you see an elf? How big is an elf? Have you ever heard a story about elves? Listen to the beginning of elf. Exaggerate the sound the "e" makes. Have the students repeat the word. Have them make the short "e" sound. Have them place their fingers on the top of their throat and make the sound and feel the vibration.

7. Put your finger on the Easter Bunny. Using your crayons, neatly color him. Discuss the picture. When do you see the Easter Bunny? What does he bring? What does he carry? Listen while I say his name. Exaggerate the "Ee" sound in Easter. The letter "Ee" is talking at the beginning. Can you hear it? What does it say? (It says "Ee" which is its name.)

8. Listen while I say the names of all the pictures. Say each one in an exaggerated fashion. Then have the students say them with you. Do all the pictures sound the same when you say them. Can you tell which pictures begin the same way. Listen carefully. Say the following pairs to your students.

   a) ear, Easter Bunny (Yes)   b) elf, egg (Yes)   c) ear, elf (No)   d) Easter Bunny, egg (No)

9. Explain to the students that the letter "Ee" can make two sounds. Say the sounds for them. Reinforce that the letter "Ee" can say its own name and sometimes makes its other sound "eh."

Auditory Game:

- Listen to these two words: **ear, eat** Do they begin the same way? (Yes) What sound do they make? (Long "Ee" says its own name)
- Listen again. (elephant, engine) Do they begin the same way? (Yes) What sound do they make? (The other sound "eh" that the letter "Ee" makes.)

Conclusion:

- Sing the alphabet song.
- Review the letters, formations, sounds, and rhymes previously taught.

E e

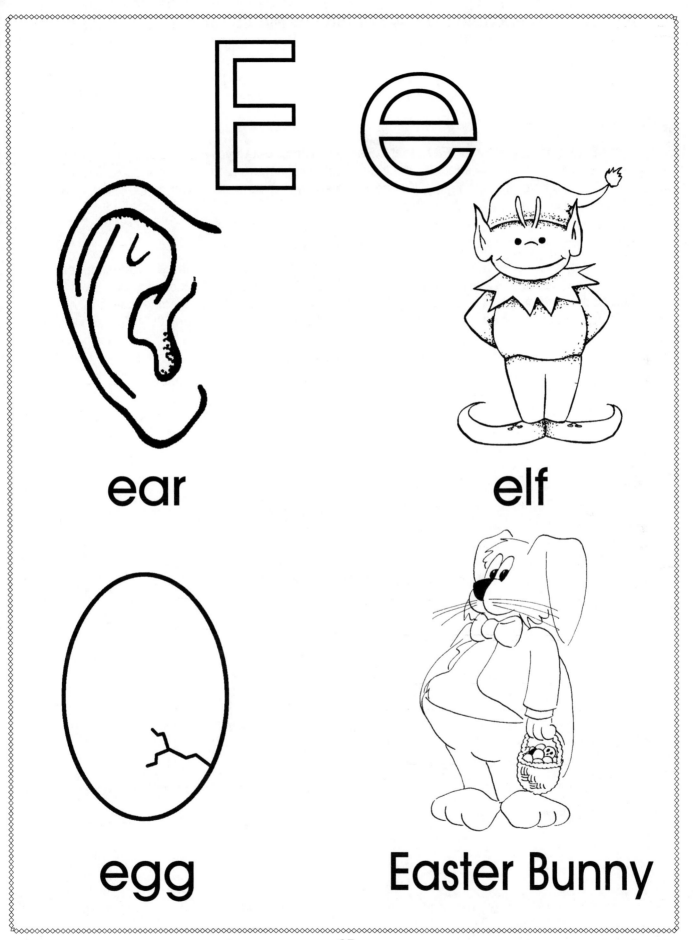

ear

elf

egg

Easter Bunny

Teaching the Recognition of the Letter "Ff"

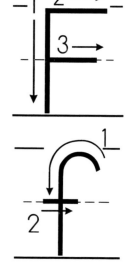

Objectives:

- To reinforce the recognition of the upper and lower case forms of the letter "Ff."
- To develop an awareness of the letter formation and how it is made.

Introduction:

Use a large alphabet card and letter "Ff" cutouts. Pass the letters out to your students allowing them to trace around the shape of the letters with their fingers to note their shapes. Discuss the types of lines in each letter noting the straight lines, curved lines, corners where they intersect, and the number of lines.

Discussion:

1. Hold up the upper case "F" and the lower case "f." Does anyone know the name for these letters? (Ff) Where do these letters live? (Point to the alphabet.) They live with 25 other letters in a big house called the alphabet. Who does the letter "Ff" live beside? (Ee) Does anyone have these letters in their names? Who has the big "F"? (Hold up the letter.) Who has the little "f"? (Hold up the letter.)

2. Talk about the shape of the upper case "F." Draw the students' attention to its straight back and two arms. Does this letter look like another letter in the alphabet that we have talked about? What is its name? (E) How is the letter "F" different from the letter "E"? (It only has two arms. One arm is missing at the bottom.) Trace its shape with your finger. Begin at the top of the vertical line. Then trace each horizontal line from the left to the right. Have your students complete the same movements on the letters that they have, in the air; on a table, and on the palm of their hands using their fingers.

3. Discuss the shape of the lower case "f." Trace the "f" to show its formation. Explain that the small "f" looks like a tall cane with a straight stick across it. It is made of a curved line that flows into a straight line. Across the line is a small straight line. Begin by making the curved line that forms the hook that flows into the straight line. Then put the line on that crosses it from left to right.

Student Activity: Alphabet Book

1. Reproduce page 29 with the letter "Ff" for your students.

2. Discuss the shapes of the letters. Encourage your students to neatly color the letters in the same directions in which they traced them.

3. Have them neatly color the fish.

4. Discuss the words that say "fish" at the bottom of the page. Have the students identify the word "Fish" with the big "F" and then have them identify the word "fish" with the little "f."

5. Glue this page into the students' alphabet scrapbook.

6. Have the students color the room in which "Ff" lives on the **Alphabet House** page.

7. Recite this rhyme with the students.

> Ff is for fish,
> Small and gold.
> Swimming in its bowl,
> Of water clean and cold.

8. Review all the letters, formations, sounds, and rhymes previously taught.

F f

Fish   fish

Teaching the Recognition of the Letter "Ff" and Its Sound

Objectives:

- To reinforce the recognition of the letter "Ff" and to introduce the sound that it makes.
- To strengthen listening skills and the ability to follow directions.
- To develop and improve communication skills.

Reproduce page 31 for your students.

Teacher Directed Activity:

1. Look at the letters at the top of the page. What are they called? (Ff)

2. Let's trace them with our fingers. Let's make them in the air. Constantly reinforce starting positions, direction in which each part flows, and left to right progression.

3. Let's look at the pictures on the page. Point to each one and say its name.

    fairy,   fire,   fox,   fork

4. Using your crayons, neatly color the fairy orange. While the students are working, discuss the picture. What is a fairy? What special things can a fairy do? Where does a fairy live? Have you ever heard of the Tooth Fairy? What special thing does she do?

5. Circle the picture of the fire with your red crayon. What does a fire do? What is used to make a fire? When would you make a fire? What kind of things can you cook over a fire?

6. Neatly color the fox with your brown crayon. What is a fox? Where does a fox live? What does a fox like to eat? Why does a farmer not like having a fox living near his farm? Have you ever seen a fox?

7. Draw a purple box around the fork. What do you use a fork for? What color is a fork? What is a fork made of?

8. Point to each picture and listen while I say each picture's name. **fairy, fire, fox, fork**
    What sound do you hear at the beginning of fairy, fox, fire, and fork? (fuh) Say the words again with me as you point to each picture. Where are your front teeth when you make the sound? (They are pressing on my bottom lip.) Put your hand in front of your mouth and say the words again. Can you feel air at the beginning of each word on your hand? The letter "Ff" is a windy sound that tickles your bottom lip. This sound is like the sound that an angry cat makes.

Auditory Game:

- Listen while I say two words: **fan, father** Do they begin the same way? (Yes)
- Listen again. This time clap your hands if the words begin with "Ff" (fuh).
- Say each group of words and wait for a response. Exaggerate the sounds at the beginning of each word.

a) forest, finger (Clap)	b) supper, fat (No clap)	c) four, five (Clap)
d) bird, five (No clap)	e) fix, find (Clap)	f) fox, six (No clap)
g) food, fan (Clap)	h) finger, hand (No clap)	i) fairy, fountain (Clap)

Conclusion:

- Sing the alphabet song.
- Review letters, formations, sounds, and rhymes previously learned

F f

fairy

fire

fox

fork

Teaching the Recognition of the Letter "Gg"

Objectives:

- To reinforce the recognition of the upper and lower case forms of the letter "Gg."
- To develop an awareness of the letter formation and how it is made.

Introduction:

Use a large alphabet card and letter "Gg" cutouts. Pass the letters out to your students allowing them to trace around the letters with their fingers to note their shapes. Discuss the types of lines in each letter noting straight lines, curved lines, corners, where they intersect, and the number of lines.

Discussion:

1. Hold up the upper and lower case "Gg." Does anyone know the name for these letters? (Gg) Where do these letters live? (Point to the alphabet.) They live with 25 other letters in a big house called the alphabet. Who do they live beside? (Ff) Does anyone have these letters in their names? Who has the big "G"? (Hold up the upper case "G.") Who has the little "g"? (Hold up the lower case "g.")

2. Explain to the students that the big "G" and the little "g" have different shapes. Talk about the shape of the upper case "G." Does it look like another letter that we have talked about? (Cc) How is it different? It is curled up farther and stops with a straight line. Trace its shape with your finger. Begin at the top and along the curved line all the way to where it stops and then make a straight line moving from the left to the right. Have your students complete the same movements on the letters that they have, in the air, on a table, and on the palm of their hands using their fingers.

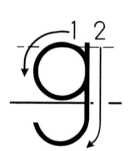

3. Discuss the shape of the lower case "g." Trace the "g" to show its formation. Explain that the small "g" looks like a ball that has a tail. Begin by making the circle and be sure to start at the top moving from the left to right. Next make the tail that kisses the ball on the right side. Practice tracing these movements to make the upper and lower case "Gg" frequently to reinforce the correct movements and positions. Constantly reinforce left to right progression and top to bottom movements.

Student Activity: Alphabet Book

1. Reproduce page 33 with the letter "Gg" for your students.

2. Discuss the shapes of the letters. Encourage your students to neatly color the letters in the same direction in which they traced them.

3. Have them neatly color the goat.

4. Discuss the words that say "goat" at the bottom of the page. Have the students identify the word "Goat" with the big "G" and then have them identify the word "goat" with the little "g."

5. Glue this page into the students' alphabet scrapbook.

6. Have the students color the room in which the letter Gg lives on the **Alphabet House** page.

7. Recite this rhyme with the students.

> Gg is for Gus the Goat,
> Standing on a bale of hay.
> I'm king of the barnyard,
> He would loudly say.

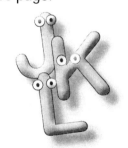

8. Review the letters, formations, sounds, and rhymes previously taught.

Goat goat

Teaching the Recognition of the Letter "Gg" and Its Sound

Objectives:

- To reinforce the recognition of the letter "Gg" and to introduce the sound that it makes.
- To strengthen listening skills and the ability to follow directions.
- To develop and improve communication skills.

Reproduce page 35 for your students.

Student Directions: (Given by the Teacher)

1. Look at the letters at the top of the page. What are they called? (Gg)

2. Let's trace them with our fingers. Let's make them in the air. Constantly reinforce starting positions, the direction in which each part flows, and left to right progression.

3. Let's look at the pictures on the page. Point to each one and say its name.

garage,   ghost,   gun,   girl

4. Put your finger on the garage. Using your crayons, neatly color the garage red and blue. While the students are working discuss the picture. What is a garage? What do people put in a garage? Do you have a garage? Do all houses have a garage?

5. Put your finger on the ghost. Using your green crayon put a circle around the ghost? What is a ghost? Have you ever seen one? What color is a ghost on Halloween? What could you use to make yourself a ghost costume? What are ghosts suppose to say?

6. Put your finger on the gun. Color the gun with your black crayon? What is a gun? What noise does a real gun make? Who wears a gun when they are at work?

7. Put your finger on the girl. Color the girl's hair yellow. What does a girl like to play with? What kinds of games do girls like to play? What kind of things do girls like to wear?

8. Point to each picture and say its name after me. Exaggerate the beginning sound as you say each word.

garage,   ghost,   gun,   girl

What sound do you hear at the beginning of each picture? (guh) When you make the sound at the beginning of garage, ghost, gun, and girl is your mouth open or closed? (open) When you make the sound where is it coming from? (It is coming from the back of my mouth or throat.) Put your hand in front of your mouth and say the words again. Can you feel air coming out of your mouth when you say the words? (Yes) Put your hand under your chin at the top of your throat. Say the words again. Can you feel your throat move? (Yes) I call this the gargling sound. Have the students make the sound guh-guh-guh.

Auditory Game:

- Listen while I say two words: **goose, gas** Exaggerate the beginning sound.
- Do they begin the same way? (Yes)
- Listen again. Raise both hands if the words that I say begin with the same sound.
- Say these pairs of words. Exaggerate the beginning sounds:

    a) gum, puppy (Hands down)   b) game, garden (Hands up)   c) jam, girl (Hands down)
    d) ghost, gold (Hands up)   e) gallop, give (Hands up)   f) girl, moose (Hands down)
    g) good, garbage (Hands up)   h) bicycle, goat (Hands down)   i) gorilla, gum (Hands up)

Conclusion:

- Sing the alphabet song.
- Review letters, formations, sounds, and rhymes previously taught.

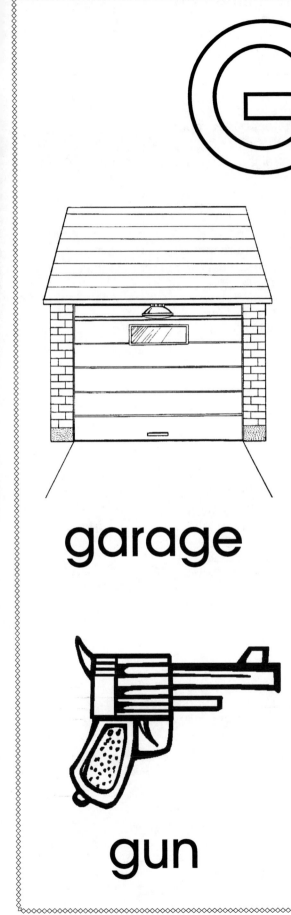

garage

ghost

gun

girl

Teaching the Recognition of the Letter "Hh"

Objectives:

- To reinforce the recognition of the upper and lower case form of the letter "Hh."
- To develop an awareness of the letter formation and how it is made.

Introduction:

Use a large alphabet card and the letter "Hh" cutouts. Pass the letters out to your students allowing them to trace around the shape of the letters with their fingers to note their shapes. Discuss the types of lines in each letter noting the straight lines, curved lines, and where the lines intersect or meet. Note also the number of lines in each letter.

Discussion:

1. Does anyone know the name for these letters. (Hold up the upper and lower case "Hh.") Where do these letters live? (Point to the alphabet.) They live with 25 other letters in a big house called the alphabet. Which letter does the "Hh" live beside? (Ee) Does anyone have these letters in their names? Who has the big "H"? (Hold up the letter.) Who has the little "h"? (Hold up the letter.)

2. Discuss the shape of the upper case "H." What are the lines like in the "H"? (Straight, two are tall, one is little.) Explain to the children that the little line holds the tall letters so that they stand straight and don't fall down. It looks something like a bridge. Trace its shape with your finger. Begin at the top of the first tall line and trace to the bottom. Take your finger away. Trace the second tall line. Begin at the top and trace it to the bottom. Take your finger away. Now trace the short line that joins the two tall lines. (Make sure the students travel from the left to the right. Have your students complete the same movements of the upper case "H" in the air, on a table, and on the palm of their hands using one finger.

3. Discuss the shape of the lower case "h." Trace the "h" to show its formation. Explain the small "h" looks somewhat like a chair. It has a straight back and a seat and a leg. Begin by making the straight back. Start at the top of the letter and travel down to the bottom. Lift off your finger. Trace the curved line that forms the seat of the chair and down the vertical line to the bottom.

Student Activity: Alphabet Book

1. Reproduce page 37 with the letter "Hh" for your students.

2. Discuss the shapes of the letters. Encourage your students to neatly color the letters in the same directions in which they have traced them.

3. Have them neatly color the horse.

4. Discuss the words that say "horse" at the bottom of the page. Have the students identify the word "Horse" with the upper case "H" and then have them identify the word "horse" with the lower case "h."

5. Glue this page into the students' alphabet scrapbook.

6. Have the students color the room in which the letter "Hh" lives on the **Alphabet House** page.

7. Recite this rhyme with the students.

Hh is for horse,
Big and tall.
Munching on hay,
In his stall.

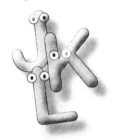

8. Review letters, formations, sounds, and rhymes previously taught.

Hh

Horse horse

Teaching the Recognition of the Letter "Hh" and Its Sound

Objectives:

- To reinforce the recognition of the letter "Hh" and to introduce the sound that it makes.
- To strengthen listening skills and the ability to follow directions.
- To develop and improve communication skills.

Reproduce page 39 for your students.

Student Directions: (Given by the Teacher)

1. Look at the letters at the top of the page. What are they called? (Hh)

2. Let's trace them with our fingers. Let's make them in the air. Constantly reinforce starting positions, the direction in which each part flows, and left to right progression.

3. Let's look at the pictures on the page. Point to each one and say its name.

   heart,   hotdog,   hook,   house

4. Using your crayons, neatly color the heart red. While the students are working discuss the picture. What is this shape called? What kinds of cards are this shape? Where else would you find a heart? What does the heart in your body do? What special day has heart-shaped cards?

5. Using your crayons neatly color the hotdog. What is a hotdog? Where are hotdogs cooked? What kinds of things do people put on their hotdogs? When do we often have hotdogs? Who likes to eat hotdogs?

6. Using your purple crayon neatly color the hook. What is a hook used for? What is a hook attached to sometimes? What is put on a hook when you go fishing? Are there different kinds of hooks? What other kinds of things are put on different hooks.

7. Neatly color the house. What do we use a house for? Are all houses the same? How are houses different? What do we call the top part of a house? How do we get in and out of a house? What do we use to see things outside the house? What kinds of rooms do you find in a house?

8. Point to each picture and say its name after me.

   heart,   hotdog,   hook,   house

What sound do you hear at the beginning of each picture? (Huh) When you make the sound at the beginning of heart, hotdog, hook, and house is your mouth open wide? (Yes) When you make this sound where is it coming from? (the back of my throat) Put your hand in front of your mouth. Say the words horse, hotdog, hook, and house again. Can you feel the air come out of your mouth when you say the words? (Yes) The letter "Hh" is a windy sound. Make the "huh" sound. I call this sound the "out of breath sound". You make this sound when you have run a long, long way.

Auditory Game:

- Listen while I say two words: **happy, hello**
- Do they begin the same way? (Yes)
- Listen again. This time put your finger on your nose if the words begin with the same sound.
- Say the following groups of words and wait for a response.

   a) heart, home (Yes)   b) catch, hatch (No)   c) hiss, harp (Yes)   d) help, hurt (Yes)
   e) bag, him (No)   g) hotdog, hamburger (Yes)   h) pump, hump (No)   i) hop, hot (Yes)
   j) Helen, hat (Yes)   k) cat, mouse (No)

Conclusion:

- Sing the alphabet song
- Review the letters, formations, sounds, and rhymes previously taught.

H h

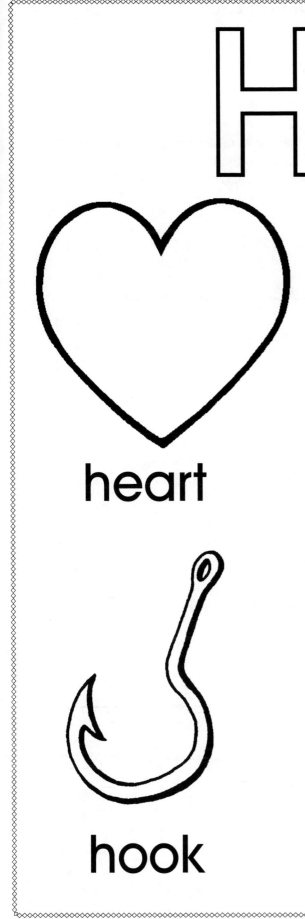

heart

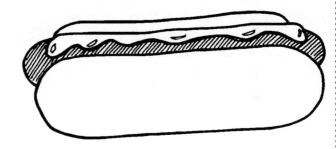

hotdog

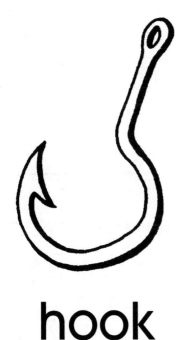

hook

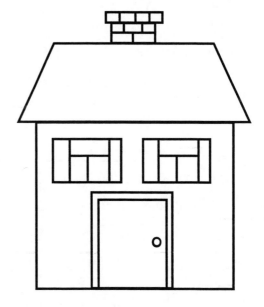

house

Teaching the Recognition of the Letter "Ii"

Objectives:

- To reinforce the recognition of the upper and lower case forms of the letter "Ii."
- To develop an awareness of the letter formation and how it is made.

Introduction:

Use a large alphabet card and the letter "Ii" cutouts. Pass out the letters to your students allowing them to trace the shape of the letters with their fingers to note their shapes. Discuss the types of lines in each one. Note the number of lines and the dot. This is the first letter that has a dot over the lower case letter.

Discussion:

1. Does anyone know the name for these letters? (Hold up the uppercase "I" and the lower case "i.") Where do these letters live? (Point to the alphabet.) They live with 25 other letters in a big house called the alphabet.) Who does the letter "Ii" live beside? (Hh) Does anyone have these letters in their names? Who has the big "I"? (Hold up the upper case "I.") Who has the little "i" in their name? (Hold up the lower case "i.")

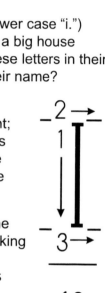

2. Discuss the shape of the upper case "I." What are the lines like in the big "I"? (straight; one is tall and two are short) Explain to the students that the letter "I" is tall and wears a hat and has a foot. Trace its shape with your fingers. Begin at the top of the tall line and trace to the bottom. Take your finger away. Trace the hat and the foot. Make sure you move from the left to the right in each case and so do your students.

3. Discuss the shape of the lower case "i." Trace the "i" to show its formation. Explain the small "i" is a straight line with a dot over it. It is half the size of the big "I." Practice making the little "i." Start at the top and travel down to the bottom. Lift off your finger. Put a dot over the top of the little line. Have your student practice tracing these movements to make both the upper and lower case letters of "Ii" frequently.

Student Activity: Alphabet Book

1. Reproduce page 41 with the letter "Ii" for your students.

2. Discuss the shapes of the letters. Encourage your students to color the letters in the same directions in which they traced them neatly.

3. Have them neatly color the ice cream cone.

4. Discuss the words that say "ice cream" at the bottom of the page. Have the students identify the words "Ice cream" with the big "I" and then have them identify the words "ice cream" with the little "i."

5. Glue this page into the students' alphabet scrapbook.

6. Have the students color the room in which the letter "Ii" lives on the **Alphabet House** page.

7. Recite this rhyme with the students.

> Ii is for ice cream,
> Everyone's favorite treat.
> It comes in all flavors,
> And tastes cold and sweet.

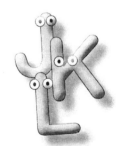

8. Review letters, formations, sounds, and rhymes previously taught.

Ice cream   ice cream

Teaching the Recognition and Sound of the Letter "Ii"

Objectives:

- To reinforce the recognition of the letter "Ii" and to introduce the sounds that it makes.
- To strengthen listening skills and the ability to follow directions.
- To develop and improve communication skills.

Reproduce page 43 for your students.

Teacher Directed Activity:

1. Look at the letters at the top of the page. What are their names? (Ii)

2. Let's make them in the air, on the paper, etc. with your finger. Remind them where to start and stop and the direction of flow.

3. Let's look at the pictures on the page. Point to each one as I say its name. Exaggerate the beginning sounds. Have the students say them again after you.

island,   igloo   ice cube,   insect

4. Use your green crayon to color the island. While the students are coloring the island discuss the picture. What is an island? Where would you find an island? How might you travel to an island? Would you like to live on an island? Why or why not? Listen to the beginning of island. Exaggerate the long "i" sound at the beginning so your students can hear it. Have them echo you. Tell them that the letter "Ii" is talking. What is it saying? (It is saying its own name.) What happens to your mouth when you say the word "island." (It opens wide.)

5. Point to the picture of the igloo. Draw a blue line under the igloo. Then color the igloo. What is an igloo? What is an igloo made from? Where might you find an igloo? Who might live in one? Listen to the beginning of "igloo." Exaggerate the sound the letter "i" makes. Have the students repeat the word. When you say the word "igloo," how is your mouth at the beginning? (It is slightly open like I am smiling.) Where does the sound come from? (back of my throat)

6. Put your finger on the ice cube. Put an orange circle around it. Now color it. What is an ice cube? What are ice cubes used for? How does an ice cube feel? Listen while I say the word. Exaggerate the long "Ii" sound. What does the "Ii" say at the beginning? (It says its own name.) Say ice cube. How is your mouth? (wide open)

7. Put your finger on the insect. Color it black and orange. What is an insect? Can you think of the names of other insects? How do insects move about? Listen while I say this picture's name. Exaggerate the short "Ii" sound. The letter "Ii" is talking and using its other sound. Can you hear it? What does it say? (ih)

8. Listen while I say the names of all the pictures. Say each word in an exaggerated fashion at the beginning. Have the students say the names too. Do all the pictures begin the same way? (No) Can you name the ones that begin the same way? (island, ice cube; igloo, insect) Explain to the students that the letter "Ii" can make two sounds. Say the long "Ii" sound. Say the short "Ii" sound.

Auditory Game:

- Listen while I say two words: **icicle, ivy**. Do they begin the same way? (Yes) Is the letter "Ii" saying its own name? (Yes) Listen while I say two more words: ink, Indian. Do they begin the same way? (Yes) Is the letter "Ii" saying its own name or its other sound? (It is saying its other sound.)
- Listen to the beginning of each word. Is it saying "i" (long sound) or "ih" (short sound)

  a) imp (ih)   b) ivory (i)   c) icing (i)   d) ignore (ih)   e) icy (i)

  f) idea (i)   g) in (ih)   h) idol (i)   i) iron (i)   j) itch (ih)

Conclusions:

- Sing the alphabet song
- Review the letters, formations, sounds, and rhymes previously taught.

I i

island

igloo

ice cube

insect

Teaching the Recognition of the Letter "Jj"

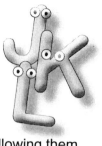

Objectives:

- To reinforce the recognition of the upper and lower case forms of the letter "Jj."
- To develop an awareness of the letter formation and how it is made.

Introduction:

Use a large alphabet card and the letter "Jj" cutouts. Pass out the letters to your students allowing them to trace around their shapes with their fingers. Discuss the types of lines in each letter noting the straight lines and the curved lines. Have them note that the small "j" has a dot over it and looks exactly like the big "J" except it hangs lower. Tell them the small letter "j" is a tail letter. Ask them if they know another letter that has a tail that they have previously talked about. (g)

Discussion:

1. Does anyone know the name for these letters? (Hold up the upper case "J" and the lower case "j.") Where do these letters live? (Point to the alphabet.) They live with 25 other letters in a big house called the alphabet. Who does the "Jj" live beside? (Ii) Does anyone have these letters in their names? Who has a big "J"? (Hold up the upper case letter "J.") Who has the little "j" in their names? (Hold up the lower case "j.")

2. Discuss the shape of the upper case "J." What are the lines like in the big "J"? (Straight with a hook. It looks like an upside down cane.) Trace its shape with your finger. Begin at the top and move your finger along the hook. Have your students complete the same movements of the upper case "J" in the air, on a table, and on the palm of their hands using one finger.

3. Discuss the shape of the lower case "j." Trace the "j" to show its formation. Explain the lower case "j" and the upper case "J" look the same except for two things. The lower case "j" hangs lower and it has a dot over it. Let's trace it. Start at the top, go along the curve and move up a little to form the hook and then stop. Now put a dot over it. Have we talked about another letter that has a dot over it? (Yes) What is its name? (i)

Student Activity: Alphabet Book

1. Reproduce page 45 with the letter "Jj" for your students.

2. Discuss the shape of each letter. Encourage your students to color the letters in the same directions in which they traced them neatly.

3. Have them neatly color the picture of jelly.

4. Discuss the words that say "jelly" at the bottom of the page. Have the students identify the word "Jelly" that has the upper case "J" and then have them identify the word "jelly" with the lower case "j".

5. Glue this page into the students' alphabet scrapbook.

6. Have the students color the room in which the letter "Jj" lives on the **Alphabet House** page.

7. Recite this rhyme with the students.

> Jj is for jelly,
> A fun food to eat.
> It shivers and shakes,
> With each bite you take.

8. Review letters, formations, sounds, and rhymes previously taught.

J j

Jelly jelly

OTM-18103 • SSR1-103 The Alphabet

Teaching the Recognition of the Letter "Jj" and Its Sound

Objectives:

- To reinforce the recognition of the letter "Jj" and to introduce the sound that it makes.
- To strengthen listening skills and the ability to follow directions.
- To develop and improve communication skills.

Reproduce page 47 for your students.

Teacher Directed Activity:

1. Look at the letters at the top of the page. What are their names? (Jj)

2. Let's trace them with our fingers. Let's make them in the air. Constantly reinforce starting positions and directions in which each letter flows.

3. Let's look at the pictures on the page. Point to each one while I say their names. Say the names with me.

jug,   jeep,   jaguar,   jacket

4. Put your finger on the jar. Using your crayons, neatly color the jar green. While the students are working discuss the picture. What is a jug? What is a jug made of? What kinds of things are sold in jugs?

5. Put your finger on the jeep. Using your yellow crayon, neatly color the jeep . What is a jeep? Who uses a jeep? Where can you drive a jeep? Do you think a jeep would be fun to ride in?

6. Put your finger on the jaguar. Neatly color it orange. What is a jaguar? Where does a jaguar live? What do you think a jaguar would like to eat? Is a jaguar a wild cat or a tame cat?

7. Put your finger on the jacket. Neatly color the jacket any color that you would like. What is a jacket? When would you wear a jacket? How are a jacket and coat different? How does a jacket usually do up?

8. Point to each picture and say its name after me.

jug,   jeep,   jaguar,   jacket

What sound do you hear at the beginning of each picture? (juh) When you make the sound at the beginning of jug, jeep, jaguar, and jacket does your mouth open? (Yes) When you make the sound where is it coming from? (the front of my mouth). This sound is like the sound that you make when you are cold and your teeth are chattering. Make the sound you make when you are cold: juh-juh-juh. Have the students make the sound quickly.

Auditory Game:

- Listen while I say two words: **jump, juice**
- Do they begin the same way? (Yes) What sound do you hear? (juh)
- Listen again. This time put you hands behind your back if the words begin with "Jj" (juh).
- Say the following groups of words and wait for a response.

a) donkey, jeans (No Response)	b) joy, June (Response)	c) gobble, job (No Response)
d) jam, jar (Response)	e) dog jumbo (No Response)	f) jester, jet (Response)
g) juicy, jello (Response)	h) goat, goose (No Response)	i) Jack, Jill (Response)

Conclusion:

- Sing the alphabet song.
- Review the letters, formations, sounds, and rhymes previously taught.

J j

jug

jeep

jaguar

jacket

Teaching the Recognition of the Letter "Kk"

Objectives:

- To reinforce the recognition of the upper and lower case forms of the letter "Kk."
- To develop an awareness of the letter formation and how it is made.

Introduction:

Use a large alphabet card and the letter "Kk" cutouts. Pass out the letters to your students allowing them to trace the letters with their fingers to note their shapes. Discuss the lines in each letter noting the straight lines and their directions. Draw to their attention that the big "K" and the little "k" look very similar.

Discussion:

1. Does anyone know the name for these letters? (Hold up the upper case "K" and the lower case "k.") (Kk) Where do these letters live? (Point to the alphabet.) They live with 25 other letters in a big house called the alphabet. In which room do they live? (They live in the room beside "Jj.") Does anyone have these letters in their names? Who has the big "K"? (Hold up the upper case "K.") Who has the little "k"? (Hold up the lower case "k.")

2. Discuss the shape of the upper case "K." What are the lines like in the big "K?" (straight, one is tall and two are short; two little ones meet the tall one in the middle) Trace its shape with your finger. Begin at the top of the tall line and travel down to the bottom. Now trace the two short lines. Begin with the top one at the top of the line and travel towards the tall line where it meets. Lift up your finger and start at the meeting place and travel along the other short line.

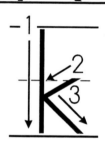

3. Discuss the shape of the lower case "k." Trace the lower case "k" to show its formation. Have your students note that in the lower case "k" the short line is being held up by the lower short line so it will stay fastened to the tall straight line. Let's trace the little "k." Start at the top, travel along the tall line to the bottom. Now make the first short line at the top. Begin at the start and travel where it is attached on the tall line. Then find the line that holds it up and begin where it is attached and travel down to the bottom.

Student Activity: Alphabet Book:

1. Reproduce page 49 with the Letter "Kk" for your students.

2. Discuss the shapes of the letters. Encourage your students to neatly color the letters in the same directions in which they traced them.

3. Have them neatly color the picture of the "kitten."

4. Discuss the words that say "kitten" at the bottom of the page. Have students identify the word "Kitten" with the upper case "K" and then have them identify the word "kitten" with the lower case "k."

5. Glue this page into the students' alphabet scrapbooks.

6. Have the students color the room in which the letter "Kk" lives on the Alphabet House page.

7. Recite this rhyme with the students.

> Kk is for kitten,
> Soft and warm.
> She is so small,
> And will do me no harm.

8. Review letters, formations, sounds, and rhymes previously taught.

K k

Kitten   kitten

Teaching the Recognition of the Letter "Kk" and Its Sound

Objectives:

- To reinforce recognition of the letter "Kk" and to introduce the sound that it makes.
- To strengthen listening skills and the ability to follow directions.
- To develop and improve communication skills.

Reproduce page 51 for your students.

Teacher Directed Activity:

1. Look at the letters at the top of the page. What are their names? (Kk)
2. Let's trace them with our fingers. Let's make them in the air. Constantly reinforce starting positions and directions in which each part of the letter flows.
3. Let's look at the pictures on the page. Point to each one as I say their names.

    kettle,   key,   kite,   kangaroo

4. Using your blue crayon neatly color the kettle. While the students are working discuss the picture. What is a kettle? What does a kettle do? What do we put inside a kettle? Why do we put water into a kettle? What does the water do inside the kettle? Why do we boil water in a kettle?
5. Using your purple crayon, neatly color the key. What is a key used for? What are keys made from? What can keys do other than opening doors? What color may a key be? Are all keys the same?
6. Neatly color the kite red and blue. What is a kite? What is a kite made of? What does a kite do? Where does it fly? What things do you need to fly a kite? Have you ever flown a kite? When is the best time to fly a kite?
7. Put your finger on the kangaroo. Color the kangaroo brown. What is a kangaroo? What can a kangaroo do? What special place does the kangaroo carry its baby? Do you know where kangaroos live? Have you ever seen a kangaroo at a zoo?
8. Point to each picture and say its name. Exaggerate the beginning sound as you say each word.

    kettle,   key,   kite,   kangaroo

What sound do you hear at the beginning of each picture. (kuh) Have the students say the names of the pictures. When you say the sound at the beginning of kettle, key, kite, and kangaroo are your lips together?(No) Where is the sound coming from? (back of my throat) This sound is made by another letter that we have talked about. Do you remember its name? (Cc) Explain to the students that the letter "Cc" and "Kk" make the coughing sound. Have the students practice making the sound.

Auditory Game:

- Listen while I say two words: **ketchup, kitchen**
- Do they begin the same way? (Yes) What sound do you hear? (kuh)
- Listen again. This time, put both of your hands on top of your head if the words begin with the same sound.
- Say the following groups of words and wait for a response.

    a) keep, dinosaur (No Response)   b) kite, kitten (Response)   c) house dog (No Response)
    d) key, kayak (Response)   e) kick, karate (Response)   f) mouse, key (No Response)
    g) Karen, Kathleen (Response)   h) Keith, Kevin (Response)   i) kangaroo, turtle (No Response)

Conclusion:

- Sing the alphabet song.
- Review letters, formations, sounds, and rhymes previously taught.

K k

kettle

key

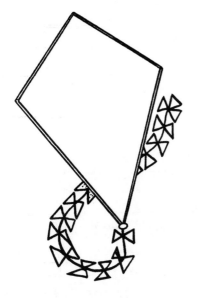

kite

kangaroo

Teaching the Recognition of the Letter "Ll"

Objectives:

- To reinforce the recognition of the upper and lower case forms of the letter "Ll."
- To develop an awareness of the letter formation and how it is made.

Introduction:

Use a large alphabet card and the letter "Ll" cutouts. Pass out the letters to your students allowing them to trace around them with their fingers to note their shapes. Discuss the lines in each letter noting the straight lines.

Discussion:

1. Does anyone know the name for these letters. (Hold up the upper case "L" and the lower case "l.") Where do these letters live? (Point to the alphabet.) They live with 25 other letters in a big house called the alphabet. Does anyone have these letters in their names? Who has the big "L"? (Hold up the upper case "L.") Who has the little "l"? (Hold up the lower case "l.")

2. Discuss the shape of the upper case "L." What are the lines like in the big "L"? (straight, one is tall, one is short) The short line is attached to the bottom of the tall line. Trace its shape with your fingers. Begin at the top of the tall line and travel down to the bottom. Take your finger away. Now put your finger on the bottom of the straight line and travel on the short line. The short line is the foot that holds the tall straight line up. Have your students complete the same movements of the upper case "L" in the air, on a table, and on the palm of their hands using one finger.

3. Discuss the shape of the lower case "l." Trace the lower case "l" to show its formation. Have your students note that the lower case "l" is only one tall line. Discuss how it is similar to the upper case "I" except it does not have a hat and a foot. Let's trace the little "l." Start at the top, travel along the tall straight line to the bottom. Trace it in the air, on the palm of your hand, on the table, etc. Have your students practice tracing the movements required to make the upper and lower case "Ll."

Student Activity: Alphabet Book

1. Reproduce page 53 with the letter "Ll" for your students.

2. Discuss the shapes of the letters. Encourage your students to color the letters neatly in the same directions in which they traced them.

3. Have them neatly color the picture of the lion.

4. Discuss the words that say "lion" at the bottom of the page. Have your students identify the word "Lion" with the upper case "L" and then have them identify the word "lion" with the lower case "l."

5. Glue this page into the students' alphabet scrapbooks.

6. Have the students color the room in which the letter "Ll" lives on the **Alphabet House** page.

7. Recite this rhyme with your students.

> Ll is for Leo Lion,
> The jungle king.
> Who growls and roars,
> At everything.

8. Review letters, formations, sounds, and rhymes previously taught.

L l

Lion   lion

Teaching the Recognition of the Letter "Ll" and Its Sound

Objectives:

- To reinforce the recognition of the letter "Ll" and to introduce the sound that it makes.
- To strengthen listening skills and the ability to follow directions.
- To develop and improve communication skills.

Reproduce page 55 for your students.

Teacher Directed Activity:

1. Look at the letters at the top of the page. What are their names? (Ll)

2. Let's trace them with our fingers. Let's make them in the air. Constantly reinforce starting positions and directions in which each part of the letter flows.

3. Let's look at the pictures on the page. Point to each one as I say their names.

   leaf,   lamp,   log,   lunch box

4. Put your finger on the leaf. Using your green crayon neatly color the leaf. While the students are working discuss the picture. What is a leaf? Where do leaves grow? What colors can leaves be? What do the leaves on trees do in the fall? Do you like to play in the leaves?

5. Put your finger on the lamp. Neatly color the lamp yellow. Discuss the picture. What is a lamp? Where would you find a lamp? What are lamps used for? Do all lamps look the same?

6. Put your finger on the log. Neatly color it black. What is a log? Where does a log come from? What could people use a log for? How might animals in the forest use a log?

7. Put your finger on the lunch box. Neatly color the lunch box using any of your crayons. What is a lunch box? How is it used? Why would children carry one to school? What kinds of things would you find in a lunch box?

8. Point to each picture and say its name. Exaggerate the beginning sound as you say each word.

   leaf,   lamp,   log,   lunch box

What sound do you hear at the beginning of each picture. (Luh) Have the student say the names of the pictures. When you say the beginning of each word where is your tongue? (It is behind my front teeth and pushes on them.) I call this the licking ice cream cone sound. You do the same thing with your tongue when you lick an ice cream cone.

Auditory Game:

- Listen while I say two words: **lemon, loon**
- Do they begin the same way? (Yes)
- Listen again. This time put your finger on your nose if the words begin with the same sound.
- Say the following groups of words and wait for a response.

   a) laugh, lump (Response)   b) monkey, hat (No Response)   c) like, lick (Response)
   d) lion, dog (No Response)   e) car, funny (No Response)   f) leopard, little (Response)
   g) kite, lilac (No Response)   h) letter, loop (Response)   i) lamb, locket (Response)

Conclusion:

- Sing the alphabet song.
- Review letters, formations, sounds, and rhymes previously taught.

L l

leaf

lamp

log

lunch box

OTM-18103 • SSR1-103 The Alphabet

Teaching the Recognition of the Letter "Mm"

Objectives:

- To reinforce the recognition of the upper and lower case forms of the letter "Mm."
- To develop an awareness of the letter formation and how it is made.

Introduction:

Use a large alphabet card and the letter "Mm" cutouts. Pass out the letters to your students allowing them to trace around them with their fingers to note their shapes. Discuss the lines in each letter noting the straight lines and the curved lines.

Discussion:

1. Does anyone know the name for these letters? (Hold up the upper case "M" and the lower case "m.") Where do these letters live? (Point to the alphabet.) They live with 25 other letters in a big house called the alphabet. Does anyone have these letters in their names? Who has the big "M"? (Hold up the upper case "M.") Who has the little "m"? (Hold up the lower case "m.")

2. Discuss the shape of the upper case "M." What are the lines like in the big "M"? (straight, slanted, have points) How many lines are there? (four) Let's trace the big "M" with your fingers. Begin at the top of the first line and travel down it. Take your finger off and put it at the top of the first line and travel down the first slanted line to the bottom. Take you finger away. Place it at the top of the other slanted line and travel down it to the bottom to form a point. Lift your finger off and place it at the top of the second slanted line. Now travel down it to the bottom. The big "M" looks like two mountains attached together.

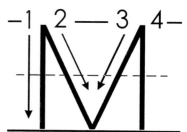

3. Discuss the shape of the lower case "m." Trace the lower case "m" to show its formation. Have your students notice that the lower case "m" is much smaller and does not look like the upper case "M." Bring to their attention that the lower case "m" has a straight line and two humps (curved lines). Have them trace the small "m" with their fingers. Start at the top of the straight line and travel down to the bottom. Lift your finger and go back to the top of the line and make the first curved line to form a hump and travel down to the bottom. Go back to the top of the first hump and make another hump and travel down to the bottom.

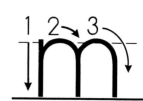

Student Activity: Alphabet Book

1. Reproduce page 57 with the letter "Mm" for your students.
2. Discuss the shapes of the letters. Encourage your students to color the letters in the same directions in which they traced them neatly.
3. Have the students neatly color the picture of the "mouse."
4. Discuss the words that say "mouse" at the bottom of the page. Have your students identify the word "Mouse" with the upper case "M" and then have them identify the word "mouse" with the lower case "m."
5. Glue this page into the students' alphabet scrapbooks.
6. Have the students color the room in which the letter "Mm" lives on the Alphabet Book page.
7. Recite this rhyme with your students.

> Mm is for mouse,
> Gray and small.
> Who lives in my house,
> Behind the wall.

8. Review the letters, formations, sounds, and rhymes previously taught.

Mm

Mouse   mouse

Teaching the Recognition of the Letter "Mm" and Its Sound

Objectives:

• To reinforce the recognition of letter "Mm" and to introduce the sound that it makes.
• To strengthen listening skills and the ability to follow directions.
• To develop and improve communications skills.

Reproduce page 59 for your students.

Teacher Directed Activity:

1. Look at the letters at the top of the page. What are they called? (Mm)

2. Let's trace them with our fingers. Let's trace them in the air. Constantly reinforce starting positions and directions in which each letter flows.

3. Let's look at the pictures on the page. Point to each one and say its name.

mat,   mask,   monkey,   moon

4. Using your red crayon, neatly color the mat. While the students are working, discuss the picture. What is a mat? What is a mat used for? Where would you find a mat? Who might like to sleep on a mat?

5. Using your black crayon, neatly color the mask. What is a mask? What do some masks look like? Why do people wear a mask? On what special day do children sometimes wear masks?

6. Neatly color the monkey with your brown crayon? What is a monkey? Where do monkeys live? Why do people like monkeys? What do monkeys eat? Where might you see a monkey?

7. Using your yellow crayon, color the moon neatly. Where do you see the moon? When do you see the moon? Does the moon always look the same? How does it look sometimes?

8. Point to the each picture and say its name after me.

mat,   mask,   monkey,   moon

What sound do you hear at the beginning of each picture? (m-m) When you make the sound at the beginning of mat, mask, monkey, and moon how are your lips? (They are squeezed or pressed together.) I call this the tasting good sound. This is the sound that we make when we see something good to eat.

Auditory Game:

• Listen to these words: **magnet, mitten**
• Do they begin the same way? (Yes) What sound do you hear? (m-m-m)
• Listen again. This time put your finger on your chin if the words begin with the sound that "Mm" makes.
• Say the following groups of words and wait for a response.

a) nose, mouth (No Response)   b) merry, muffin (Response)   c) jam, meat (No Response)
d) moose, mole (Response)   e) mountain, music (Response)   f) mail, miner (Response)
g) nut, muffin (No Response)   h) Michael, Mary (Response)   i) button, man (No Response)

Conclusion:

• Sing the alphabet song.
• Review the letters, formations, sounds, and rhymes that have been previously taught.

M m

mat

mask

monkey

moon

Teaching the Recognition of the Letter "Nn"

Objectives:

- To reinforce the recognition of the upper and lower case "Nn."
- To develop an awareness of the letter formation and how it is made.

Introduction:

Use a large alphabet card and the letter "Nn" cutouts. Pass out the letters to your students allowing them to trace around them with their fingers to note their shapes. Discuss the lines in each letter noting the straight lines and the curved lines.

Discussion:

1. Does anyone know the name for these letters? (Hold up the upper case "N" and the lower case "n.") Where do these letters live? (Point to the alphabet.) They live with 25 other letters in a big house called the alphabet. Who does the letter "Nn" live beside? (Mm) Does anyone have these letters in their names? Who has the big "N"? (Hold up the upper case "N.") Who has the little "n"? (Hold up the lower case "n.")

2. Discuss the shape of the upper case "N." What are the lines like in the big "N"? (straight slanted) How many lines are there? (three) Let's trace the big "N" with our fingers. Begin at the top of the first line and travel down it. Take your finger off and put it at the top of the first line and travel down the first slanted line to the bottom. Take your finger away. Place it at the top again. Trace along the last straight line to the bottom. Does the letter "Nn" look similar to another letter that we have talked about. (Yes) What is its name? (Mm) How are the big "M" and "N" different? (The big "N" has only three lines, the big "M" has four lines.)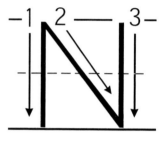

3. Discuss the shape of the lower case "n." Trace the lower case "n" to show its formation. Have your students notice that the lower case "n" is much smaller and does not look like the upper case "N." Bring to their attention that the lower case "n" has a straight line and only one hump (curved line). Have them trace the small "n" with their fingers. Start at the top of the straight line and travel to the bottom. Lift your finger and make the curved line to form the hump and travel down the straight line to the bottom.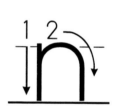

Student Activity: Alphabet Book

1. Reproduce page 61 with the letter "Nn" for your students.

2. Discuss the shapes of the letters. Encourage your students to color the letters in the same directions in which they traced them.

3. Have the students neatly color the picture of the "nest."

4. Discuss the words that say "nest" at the bottom of the page. Have your students identify the word "Nest" with the upper case "N" and then identify the word "nest" with the lower case "n."

5. Glue this page into the students' alphabet scrapbooks.

6. Have the students color the room in which the letter "Nn" lives on the **Alphabet House** page.

7. Recite this rhyme with your students.

> Nn is for nest,
> Built high in a tree.
> Among the leaves,
> So no one can see.

8. Review letters, formations, sounds, and rhymes previously taught.

N n

Nest   nest

Teaching the Recognition of the Letter "Nn" and Its Sound

Objectives:

- To reinforce the recognition of the letter "Nn" and to introduce the sound that it makes.
- To strengthen listening skills and the ability to follow directions.
- To develop and improve communication skills.

Reproduce page 63 for your students.

Teacher Directed Activity:

1. Look at the letters at the top of the page. What are they called? (Nn)

2. Let's trace them with our fingers. Let's trace them in the air. Constantly reinforce starting positions and directions in which each letter flows.

3. Let's look at the pictures on the page. Point to each one and say its name.

nail,   net,   nose,   nut

4. Using your black crayon, circle the nail. Neatly color it. What is a nail? What is it made of? What is it used for? What tool do you use to make a nail stay in wood?

5. Put a green box around the net. What is a net used for? What kinds of things can you catch with a net? Have you ever tried to catch something using a net?

6. Draw a red line under the nose. What is a nose? What is it used for? Where is it on your body? Do animals have noses? What do they use them for?

7. Neatly color the nut brown? What is a nut? What part of a nut do you eat? What part do you not eat? Where do some nuts grow? Can you think of an animal that likes to eat nuts?

8. Point to each picture and say its name after me.

nail,   net,   nose,   nut

What sound do you hear at the beginning of each picture? (n-n) When you make the sound at the beginning of nail, net, nose, and nut where is your tongue? (It is pressing on the back of my front teeth.) I call this sound the "tickling my nose sound." When you make the sound it tickles your nose.

Auditory Game:

- Listen to these words: **name, nine**
- Do they begin the same way? (Yes) What sound do you hear? (n-n-n)
- Listen again. This time put your finger on your nose if the words begin with the sound that "Nn" makes.
- Say the following groups of words and wait for a response.

a) moon, nut (No Response)	b) nice, noise (Response)	c) nickel, dime (No Response)
d) night, new (Response)	e) pop, nine (No response)	f) number, neat (Response)
g) needle, doctor (No Response)	h) nap, need (Response)	i) nurse, nest (Response)

Conclusion:

- Sing the alphabet song.
- Review the letters, formations, sounds, and rhymes that have been previously taught.

N n

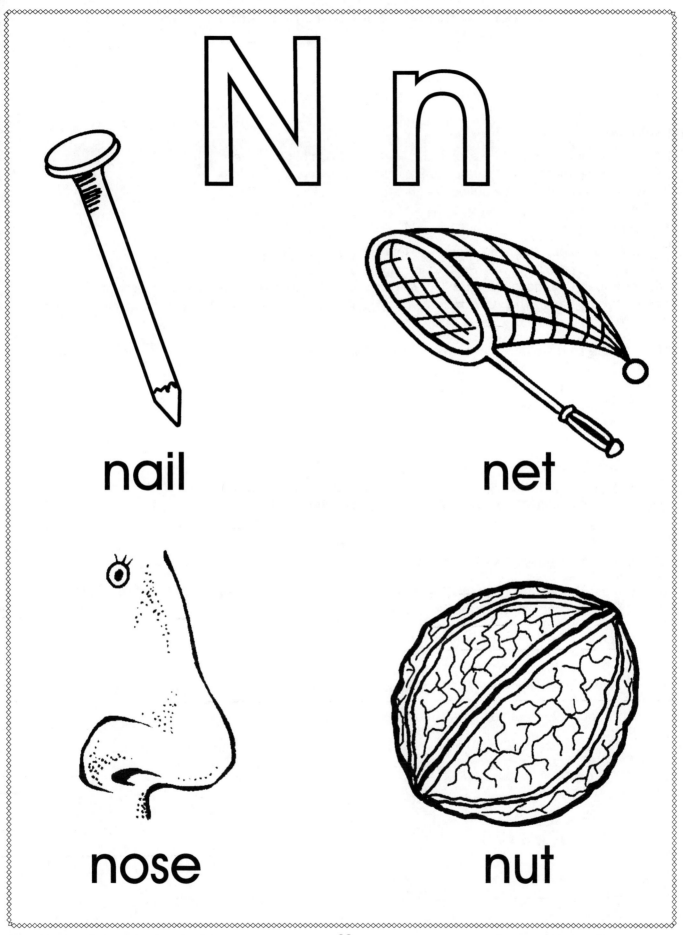

nail

net

nose

nut

Teaching the Recognition of the Letter "Oo"

Objectives:

- To reinforce the recognition of the upper and lower case "Oo."
- To develop an awareness of the letter formation and how it is made.

Introduction:

Use a large alphabet card and the letter "Oo" cutouts. Pass out the letters to your students allowing them to trace around them with their fingers to note their shapes. Discuss the lines in each letter noting the curved lines.

Discussion:

1. Does anyone know the names for these letters? (Hold up the upper case "O" and the lower case "o.") Where do these letters live? (Point to the alphabet.) They live with 25 other letters in a big house called the alphabet. Who does the letter "Oo" live beside? (Nn) Does anyone have these letters in their names? Who has the big "O"? (Hold up the upper case "O.") Who has the little "o"? (Hold up the lower case "o.")

2. Discuss the shape of the upper case "O." What are the lines like in the big letter "O." (One big curved line or a circle) Let's trace the big "O" with our fingers. Begin at the top of the circle. Watch while I trace the letter. Now you trace its shape. Make sure the students travel from left to right and back to where they started.

3. Discuss the shape of the lower case "o." Have your students notice they are the same shape. How is the little "o" and the big "O" different? (One is smaller.) Tell the students that the big "O" and the little "o" are made exactly the same way. Practice making the letters. Stress the flow and the directions.

Student Activity: Alphabet Book

1. Reproduce page 65 with the letter "Oo" for your students.

2. Discuss the shapes of the letters. Encourage your students to color the letters in the same direction in which they traced them.

3. Have the students neatly color the picture of the "orange."

4. Discuss the words that say "orange" at the bottom of the page. Have your students identify the word "Orange" with the upper case "O." Then have them identify the word "orange" with the lower case "o."

5. Glue this page into the students' alphabet scrapbooks.

6. Have the students color the room in which the "Oo" lives on the **Alphabet House** page.

7. Recite this rhyme with your students.

> "Oo" is for orange,
> A fruit juicy and sweet.
> It grows on a tree,
> And is a healthy treat.

8. Review letters, formations, sounds, and rhymes previously taught.

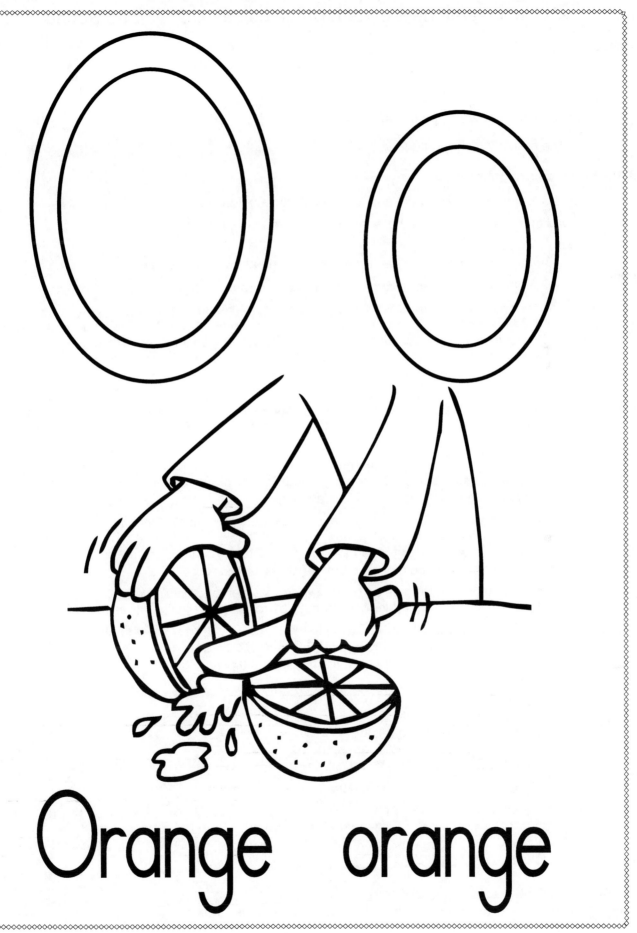

Orange   orange

Teaching the Recognition of the Letter "Oo" and Its Sound

Objectives:

- To reinforce the recognition of the letter "Oo" and to introduce the sounds that it makes.
- To strengthen listening skills and the ability to follow directions.
- To develop and improve communication skills.

Reproduce page 67 for your students.

Teacher Directed Activity:

1. Look at the letters at the top of the page. What are they called? (Oo)
2. Let's trace them with our fingers. Let's trace them in the air. Constantly reinforce the left to right progression.
3. Let's look at the pictures on the page. Point to each one and say its name.

opossum,   octopus,   ocean,   otter

4. Put your finger on the opossum. Color the opossum gray. While the students are working discuss the picture. Do you know what an opossum is? Where would one live? What special thing can the opossum do with its tail? Listen while I say the word "opossum". Exaggerate the long "o" sound at the beginning. Explain that the letter "Oo" is talking. What is it saying? (It's saying its own name.) Have the students say the word "opossum." What shape is your mouth at the beginning of the word? (round like an "o")
5. Put your finger on the octopus. Color the octopus pink. What is an octopus? Where does one live? How many tentacles or arms does an octopus have? What do you think an octopus uses his tentacles for?
6. Listen while I say "octopus." Exaggerate the short "o" sound. Explain that the letter "o" is making its other sound. Have the students say "octopus." What is your mouth like at the beginning of octopus? (wide open) What sound does the "o" make? (aw)
7. Put your finger on the ocean. Color the ocean blue. What is an ocean? What lives in an ocean? Have you ever swam in an ocean? Listen while I say the word "ocean." Exaggerate the long "o" sound. What is the "o" saying at the beginning of "ocean." (It is saying its own name.) Have the students say the word "ocean." What is the shape of your mouth? (round like an "o")
8. Neatly color the otter brown. What is an otter? Where does an otter live? How does this otter like to swim? Say the word "otter." What does you mouth do? (opens wide) What does the "Oo" say? (aw)
9. Say the words "opossum, ocean." Do they begin the same way? (Yes) What sound do you hear? (the letter "O's" name) Say the words "octopus, otter." Do they begin the same way? (Yes) What sound do you hear? (aw) Explain again to your students that sometimes the letter "Oo" says its own name and sometimes it says "aw."

Auditory Game:

- Listen to the words that I am going to say.
  If you hear them say "O" at the beginning, stand up.
  If you hear them say "aw" at the beginning, sit down.

- Say each pair of words and wait for a response.

a) open, only (Stand Up)	b) on, off (Sit Down)	c) ocean, okay (Stand Up)
d) olive, odd (Sit Down)	e) oak, oar (Stand Up)	f) oboe, odour (Stand Up)
g) old, oval (Stand Up)	h) Oscar, ostrich (Sit Down)	i) over, open (Stand Up)

Conclusion:

- Sing the alphabet song.
- Review the letters, formations, sounds, and rhymes previously taught.

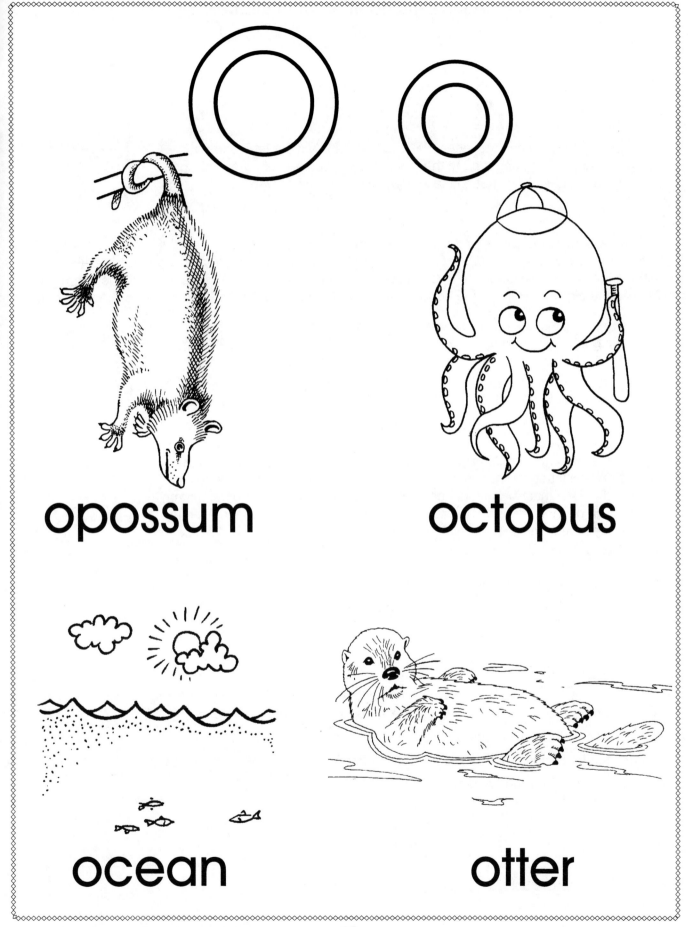

opossum

octopus

ocean

otter

Teaching the Recognition of the Letter "Pp"

Objectives:

- To reinforce the recognition of the upper and lower case "Pp."
- To develop an awareness of the letter formation and how it is made.

Introduction:

Use a large alphabet card and the letter "Pp" cutouts. Pass out the letters to your students allowing them to trace around them with their fingers to note their shapes. Discuss the lines in each letter noting the straight lines and the curved lines.

Discussion:

1. Does anyone know the name for these letters? (Hold up the upper case "P" and the lower case "p.") Where do these letters live? (Point to the alphabet.) They live with 25 letters in a big house called the alphabet. Who does the letter "Pp" live beside? (Oo) Does anyone have these letters in their names? Who has the big "P"? (Hold up the upper case "P.") Who has the little "p"? (Hold up the lower case "p.")

2. Discuss the shape of the upper case "P." What are the lines like in the big "P?" (One is straight. One is curved.) Let's trace the big "P" with our fingers. Begin at the top of the straight line and travel to the bottom. Lift your finger off and put it at the top of the straight line. Move away from the line to make a fat curved line that looks like half of a ball joined to the line.

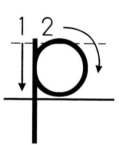

3. Discuss the shape of the lower case "p." Trace the lower case "p" to show its formation. Make the students aware that the upper case "P" and the lower case "p" look alike but one stands taller than the other. Explain to them that the lower case "p" is a tail letter and hangs down. Make sure the students form the letter "p" correctly. Have them start at the top of the straight line and travel to the bottom. Then they lift off their finger and place it near the straight line and make a circle that travels towards the line, kisses it and travels up to close the circle. Practice making both letters in the air, on a table, etc.

Student Activity: Alphabet Book

1. Reproduce page 69 with the letter "Pp" for your students.

2. Discuss the shapes of the letters. Encourage your students to color the letters in the same directions in which they traced them.

3. Have the students neatly color the picture of the "pig."

4. Discuss the words that say "pig" at the bottom of the page. Have your students identify the word "Pig" with the upper case "P" and then identify the word "pig" with the lower case "p."

5. Glue this page into the students' alphabet scrapbooks.

6. Have the students color the room in which the letter "Pp" lives on the **Alphabet House** page.

7. Recite this rhyme with your students.

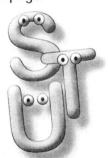

> Pp is for Pig,
> Fat and pink.
> Who squeals and oinks,
> While he eats and drinks.

8. Review letters, formations, sounds, and rhymes previously taught.

P p

Pig   pig

Teaching the Recognition of the Letter "Pp" and Its Sound

Objectives:

- To reinforce the recognition of the letter "Pp" and to introduce the sound that it makes.
- To strengthen listening skills and the ability to follow directions.
- To develop and improve communication skills.

Reproduce page 71 for your students.

Teacher Directed Activity:

1. Look at the letters at the top of the page. What are they called? (Pp)
2. Let's trace them with our fingers. Let's trace them in the air. Constantly reinforce starting positions and directions in which each letter flows.
3. Let's look at the pictures on the page. Point to each one and say its name.

pail,   pencil,   pumpkin,   pool

4. Using your green crayon neatly color the pail. While the students are working discuss the picture. What is a pail? What is a pail used for? What kinds of things can you put in a pail? Where would you play with a pail? Who carried a pail up to a well to get some water?
5. Put your finger on the pencil. Neatly color the pencil using your yellow crayon. What is a pencil used for? What is a pencil made of? What do you do with a pencil to make it write better? Are all pencils yellow? What can some pencils do?
6. Color the pumpkin orange. What is a pumpkin? Where do pumpkins grow? What can we make using a pumpkin? What can your mother make with a pumpkin? On what special night do we use pumpkins as a light?
7. Color the water in the pool blue. What is a pool? What can you do in a pool? Where do people put a pool? Do you have a pool? When do we use a pool?
8. Point to each picture and say its name after me.

pail,   pencil,   pumpkin,   pool

What sound do you hear at the beginning of each word? (puh) When you make the sound at the beginning of pail, pencil, pumpkin, and pool how are your lips? (Pressed together.) Put your hand in front of your mouth and say the words again. What comes out of your mouth when you first say each one? (a blast of air) I call this sound the popcorn popping sound. It makes the same sound that popcorn makes when it is popping.

Auditory Game:

- Listen to these words: **porridge, purple**
- Do they begin the same way? (Yes) What sound do you hear? (puh)
- Listen again. This time clap your hands if the word that I say begins like "pig."
- Say the following words and wait for a response.

<table>
<tr><td>a) pig, door (No Response)</td><td>b) pig, pack (Response)</td><td>c) pig, mouse (No Response)</td></tr>
<tr><td>d) pig, pen (Response)</td><td>e) pig, house (No Response)</td><td>f) pig, penny (Response)</td></tr>
<tr><td>g) pig, pancakes (Response)</td><td>h) pig, party (Response)</td><td>i) pig, push (Response)</td></tr>
</table>

Conclusion:

- Review the letters, formations, sounds, and rhymes that have been previously taught.

P p

pail

pencil

pumpkin

pool

Teaching the Recognition of the Letter "Qq"

Objectives:

- To reinforce the recognition of the upper and lower case "Qq."
- To develop an awareness of the letter formation and how it is made.

Introduction:

Use a large alphabet card and the letter "Qq" cutouts. Pass out the letters to your students allowing them to trace around them with their fingers to note their shapes. Discuss the lines in each letter noting curved lines, straight lines, and circular ones.

Discussion:

1. Does anyone know the name for these letters? (Hold up the upper case "Q" and the lower case "q.") Where do these letters live? (Point to the alphabet.) They live with 25 other letters in a big house called the alphabet. Who does the letter "Qq" live beside? (Pp) Does anyone have these letters in their names? Who has the big "Q"? (Hold up the upper case "Q.") Who has the little "q"? Hold up the lower case "q.")

2. Discuss the shape of the upper case "Q." What are the lines like in the big "Q"? (round, curved, circle, little line) Let's trace the big "Q" with our fingers. Begin at the top of the circle and move along the line back to where you started. Now put your finger on the top of the little line that crosses the circle and travel down it to the bottom. Stress left to right progression while making the circular line. Practice making the upper case "Q" in the air, on the table, and on the palm of your hand. What other letter in the alphabet does the big "Q" look like? (the big "O") How are the big "O" and the big "Q" different? (The "Q" has a little stick crossing the circle.)

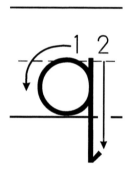

3. Discuss the shape of the lower case "q." Trace the lower case "q" to show its formation. When we make the little "q" first we make a letter "o." Demonstrate making the "o." Make sure that you move from the left to the right. Next, we make the straight line that kisses the ball on its right side. Practice tracing the little "q" in the air, on a table, and on the palm of your hand. The little "q" is a tail letter. What other letters have tails that we have talked about? (g,j,p) Do their tails look the same? (No)

Student Activity: Alphabet Book

1. Reproduce page 73 with the letter "Qq" for your students.
2. Discuss the shapes of the letters. Encourage your students to color the letters in the same direction in which they traced them.
3. Have the students neatly color the "queen."
4. Discuss the words that say "queen" at the bottom of the page. Have your students identify the word "Queen" with the upper case "Q" and then identify the word "queen" with the lower case "q."
5. Glue this page into the students' alphabet scrapbooks.
6. Have the students color the room in which the letter "Qq" lives on the **Alphabet House** page.
7. Recite this rhyme with your students.

> Qq is for Queen,
> A lady so fine.
> Who wears a crown,
> While she dines.

8. Review letters, formations, sounds, and rhymes previously taught.

Queen   queen

Teaching the Recognition of the Letter "Qq" and Its Sound

Objectives:

- To reinforce the recognition of the letter "Qq" and to introduce the sound that it makes.
- To strengthen listening skills and the ability to follow directions.
- To develop and improve communication skills.

Reproduce page 75 for your students.

Teacher Directed Activity:

1. Look at the letters at the top of the page. What are they called? (Qq)

2. Let's trace them with our fingers. Remember where to start and stop. Let's trace them in the air. Constantly reinforce starting positions and directions in which each letter flows.

3. Let's look at the pictures on the page. Point to each one and say its name.

   quarter,   quilt,   quill,   quiet

4. Put your finger on the quarter. Draw a red line under it. Now neatly color it. Discuss the picture while the students are working. What is a quarter? What would you do with one? What is a quarter made of? What color is it?

5. Put your finger on the quill. Color the quill a pretty color. What was a quill used for? What does a quill look like? Where do you think it came from? Do we use quill pens today? When did they use a quill pen?

6. Put your finger on the quilt. Neatly color it. What is a quilt? Have you ever seen one? What is another name for a quilt? How are quilts made? When did mothers have to make their own quilts?

7. Put your finger on the person who is saying quiet. Draw a blue box around the picture. Why would someone tell you to be quiet? When should people be quiet? In what kind of places do people have to be quiet?

8. Point to each picture and say its name after me.

   quarter,   quilt,   quill,   quiet

   What sound do you hear at the beginning of each picture? (quh) When you make the sound at the beginning of quarter, quilt, quill, and quiet what does you mouth do? (It makes my lips squeeze together into an O.) Put your hand in front of your mouth. Say quilt. What do you feel? (air) "Qq" is a windy sound. What other sounds are windy too that we have talked about. (b, c, f, h, p)

Auditory Game:

- Listen to this word: **quart**
- Does it start with the letter "Qq?" (Yes)
- Listen again. If the word that I say begins like queen, put your hand over your mouth.
- Say the following words.

   a) butter (No Response)   b) quack (Response)   c) pumpkin (No Response)
   d) quiver (Response)   e) quake (Response)   f) dog (No Response)
   g) quit (Response)   h) muffin (No Response) i) quick (Response)

Conclusion:

- Review the letters, formations, sounds, and rhymes that have been previously taught.

Q q

quarter

quilt

quill

quiet

Teaching the Recognition of the Letter "Rr"

Objectives:

- To reinforce the recognition of the upper and lower case "Rr."
- To develop an awareness of the letter formation and how it is made.

Introduction:

Use a large alphabet card and the letter "Rr" cutouts. Pass out the letters to your students allowing them to trace around them with their fingers to note their shapes. Discuss the lines in each letter noting the straight lines and the curved lines.

Discussion:

1. Does anyone know the name for these letters? (Hold up the upper case "R" and the lower case "r.") Where do these letters live? (Point to the alphabet.) They live with 25 other letters in a big house called the alphabet. Who does the letter "Rr" live beside? (Qq) Does anyone have these letters in their names? Who has the big "R"? (Hold up the upper case "R.") Who has the little "r"? (Hold up the lower case "r.")

2. Discuss the shape of the upper case "R." What are the lines like in the big "R?" (straight, curved, slanted, short, tall) How many lines are there? (three) Let's trace the big "R" with our fingers. Begin at the top of the big line and travel down it to the bottom. Take your finger off and place it at the top of the big line. Now trace the curved line to where it meets the big line. Next travel down the straight slanted line to the bottom. Let's trace it again in the air, on a table, and on the palm of your hand.

3. Discuss the shape of the lower case "r." Trace its shape to show its formation. Have your students notice that the little "r" is half the size of the big "R" and they do not look at all alike. Bring to their attention that the little "r" is made of a small straight line and a small curved line. Have them trace the small "r" with their fingers. Start at the top of the little line and travel to the bottom. Take your finger away and place it slightly below the top of the straight line and travel away from it to make the little curved line or hook. Practice making both letters in a variety of places.

Student Activity: Alphabet Book

1. Reproduce page 77 with the letter "Rr" for your students.

2. Discuss the shapes of the letters. Encourage your students to neatly color the letters in the same directions in which they traced them

3. Have the students neatly color the picture of the "raccoon."

4. Discuss the words that say "raccoon" at the bottom of the page. Have your students identify the word "Raccoon" with the upper case "R" and then identify the word "raccoon" with the lower case "r."

5. Glue this page into the students' alphabet scrapbooks.

6. Have the students color the room in which the letter "Rr" lives on the **Alphabet House** page

7. Recite this rhyme with your students.

> Rr is for raccoon,
> Who looks for food.
> Late at night,
> By the light of the moon.

8. Review letters, formations, sounds, and rhymes previously taught.

Raccoon raccoon

Teaching the Recognition of the Letter "Rr" and Its Sound

Objectives:

- To reinforce the recognition of the letter "Rr" and to introduce the sound that it makes.
- To strengthen listening skills and the ability to follow directions.
- To develop and improve communication skills.

Reproduce page 79 for your students.

Teacher Directed Activity:

1. Look at the letters at the top of the page. What are they called? (Rr)

2. Let's trace them with our fingers. Let's trace them in the air. Constantly reinforce starting positions and directions in which each letter flows.

3. Let's look at the pictures on the page. Point to each one and say its name.

   rain,   rabbit,   ring,   rocket

4. Put your finger on the picture of rain. Color the umbrella red. Color the raindrops blue. While the students are working, discuss the picture. What is an umbrella? Why do we use one? Where does the rain come from? What is rain made of? Why are people happy when it rains?

5. Put your finger on the rabbit. Color the rabbit brown. What is a rabbit? Where does a rabbit live? What does a rabbit like to eat? How does a rabbit move? Do you know the name of a storybook rabbit?

6. Put your finger on the ring. Draw a green line under it. Color the ring any color. What is a ring? Where do people wear rings? Do all rings look the same? What makes a ring pretty? Do you have a ring?

7. Put your finger on the rocket. Color it purple. What is a rocket? Where might a rocket go? Who travels in a rocket?

8. Point to each picture and say its name after me.

   rain,   rabbit,   ring,   rocket

   What sound do you hear at the beginning of each picture? (r-r) When you make the sound at the beginning of rain, rabbit, ring, and rocket where is the sound coming from in your mouth? (back of my mouth or throat) What does this sound remind you of? (Answers will vary.) The sound that "Rr" makes reminds me of a dog who is angry and is growling. I call this sound the angry dog sound.

Auditory Game:

- Listen to these words: **robin, reindeer**
- Do they begin the same way? (Yes) What sound do you hear at the beginning? (r-r-r)
- Listen again. This time put your hands on your shoulders if the words begin with the sound that "Rr" makes.
- Say the following groups of words and wait for a response.

  a) rabbit, roof (Response)   b) water, paper (No Response)   c) rug, robber (Response)
  d) ring, doctor (No Response)   e) ball, cookie (No Response)   f) ribbon, riding (Response)
  g) read, walk (No Response)   h) radio, rest (Response)   i) loon, picture (No Response)

Conclusion:

- Review the letters, formation, sounds, and rhymes that have been previously taught.

R r

rain

rabbit

ring

rocket

OTM-18103 • SSR1-103 The Alphabet

Teaching the Recognition of the Letter "Ss"

Objectives:

- To reinforce the recognition of the upper and lower case "Ss."
- To develop an awareness of the letter formation and how it is made.

Introduction:

Use a large alphabet card and the letter "Ss" cutouts. Pass out the letters to your students allowing them to trace around them with their fingers to note their shapes. Discuss the lines in each letter noting the curves.

Discussion:

1. Does anyone know the name for these letters? (Hold up the upper case "S" and the lower case "s.") Where do these letters live? (Point to the alphabet.) They live with 25 other letters in a big house called the alphabet. Who does the letter "Ss" live beside? (Rr) Does anyone have these letters in their name? Who has the big "S"? (Hold up the upper case "S.") Who has the little "s"? (Hold up the lower case "s.")

2. Discuss the shape of the upper case "S". What are the lines like in the big "S"? (curvy; like a snake) How many lines are there? (one) Let's trace the big "S" with our fingers. Begin at the top of the line and travel down the curvy path to where it stops. This letter is made in one movement.

3. Discuss the shape of the little "s." Have your students note that the big "S" and the little "s" look exactly the same. What is the difference between the big "S" and the little "s." (One is bigger) Which one is the biggest? (the big "S") Make sure the students are aware that both letters are made exactly the same way. Practice making both letters in the air, on a table, and on the palm of your hand.

Student Activity: Alphabet Book

1. Reproduce page 81 with the letter "Ss" for your students.

2. Discuss the shapes of the letters. Encourage your students to color the letters in the same direction in which they traced them.

3. Have the students neatly color the picture of the "seal."

4. Discuss the words that say "seal" at the bottom of the page. Have your students identify the word "Seal" with the upper case "S" and then identify the word "seal" with the lower case "s."

5. Glue this page into the students' alphabet scrapbooks.

6. Have the students color the room in which the letter "Ss" lives on the **Alphabet House** page.

7. Recite this rhyme with your students.

> Ss is for Sammy Seal,
> Waiting for something nice.
> To make a tasty meal,
> Hiding under the ice.

8. Review letters, formations, sounds, and rhymes previously taught.

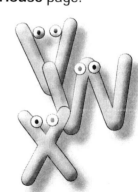

S s

Seal   seal

Teaching the Recognition of the Letter "Ss" and Its Sound

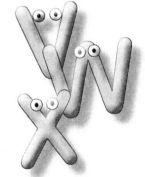

Objectives:

- To reinforce the recognition of the letter "Ss" and to introduce the sound that it makes.
- To strengthen listening skills and the ability to follow directions.
- To develop and improve communication skills.

Reproduce page 83 for your students.

Teacher Directed Activity:

1. Look at the letters at the top of the page. What are they called? (Ss)
2. Let's trace them with our fingers. Let's trace them in the air. Constantly reinforce starting positions and directions in which each letter flows.
3. Let's look at the pictures on the page. Point to each one and say its name.

sack,   Santa,   sun,   seeds

4. Put your finger on the sack. Color it yellow. While the students are working, discuss the picture. What is a sack? What is a sack used for? What kinds of things could be found in a sack.
5. Put your finger on the picture of Santa. Color him neatly. Who is Santa? When do we see him? What does he bring? Where does he live?
6. Draw a black line under the sun. Color the sun yellow. What is the sun? Where do you see the sun? When do you see the sun? How do you feel in the sun? How does the sun help us?
7. Neatly color the seeds any color. What are seeds used for? Where do we plant seeds? What kinds of things grow from seeds?
8. Point to each picture and say its name after me.

sack,   Santa,   sun,   seeds

What sound do you hear at the beginning of each picture? (s-s-s) When you make this sound how is your mouth? (It is open a little.) How are your teeth? (slightly together) Where is your tongue? (behind my teeth) I call this the Sammy Snake hissing sound. It is like the sound a snake makes when it is afraid.

Auditory Game:

- Listen to these words: **Sandra, Susan**
- Do they begin the same way? (Yes) What sound do you hear? (s-s-s)
- Listen again. This time shake your head yes if the words begin the same way.
- Say the following groups of words and wait for a response.

a) see, come (No Response)
b) Sunday, Saturday (Response)
c) puppy, skunk (No Response)
d) summer, something (Response)
e) soap, socks (Response)
f) roof, sidewalk (No Response)
g) soup, sandwich (Response)
h) plane, car (No Response)
i) sound, silver (Response)

Conclusion:

- Review the letters, formations, sounds, and rhymes that have been previously taught.

S s

sack

Santa

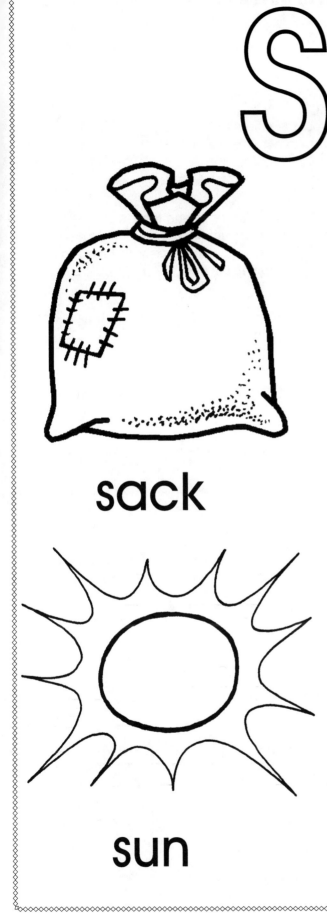

sun

seeds

 OTM-18103 • SSR1-103 The Alphabet

Teaching the Recognition of the Letter "Tt"

Objectives:

- To reinforce the recognition of the upper and lower case "Tt."
- To develop an awareness of the letter formation and how it is made.

Introduction:

Use a large alphabet card and the letter "Tt" cutouts. Pass out the letters to your students allowing them to trace around them with their fingers to note their shapes. Discuss the type of lines in each letter.

Discussion:

1. Does anyone know the name for these letters? (Hold up the upper case "T" and the lower case "t.") Where do these letters live? (Point to the alphabet.) They live with 25 other letters in a big house called the alphabet. Who does the letter "Tt" live beside? (Ss) Does anyone have these letters in their names? Who has the big "T"? (Hold up the upper case "T.") Who has the little "t"? (Hold up the lower case "t.")

2. Discuss the shape of the upper case "T." What are the lines like in the big "T"? (straight) How many lines are there? (two) Let's trace the big "T" with our fingers. Begin at the end of the first line and travel across it and then stop. Make sure the students travel from left to right. Now put your finger on the top of the tall line and travel down to the bottom. Practice tracing the upper case "T" in a variety of ways.

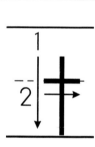

3. Discuss the shape of the lower case "t." Have the students note that the two letters look similar. Tell them that the little "t" looks like a telephone or hydro pole. Let's trace the little "t." Begin at the top of the tall line and travel down it to the bottom and stop. Take your finger away and place it on the line that crosses the tall line. Make sure the students travel from left to right. Now travel across this line. Practice making the upper and lower "Tt" in a variety of ways.

Student Activity: Alphabet Book

1. Reproduce page 85 with the letter "Tt" for your students.

2. Discuss the shapes of the letters. Encourage your students to color the letters in the same directions in which they traced them.

3. Have the students neatly color the picture of the "turtle."

4. Discuss the words that say "turtle" at the bottom of the page. Have your students identify the word "turtle" with the upper case "T" and then identify the word "turtle" with the lower case "t."

5. Glue this page into the students' alphabet scrapbooks.

6. Have the students color the room in which the letter "Tt" lives on the **Alphabet House** page.

7. Recite this rhyme with your students.

> Tt is for Tom Turtle,
> Small and green.
> Hides in his shell,
> Where he can't be seen.

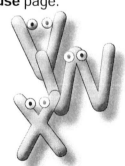

8. Review letters, formations, sounds, and rhymes previously taught.

T t

Turtle   turtle

 OTM-18103 • SSR1-103 The Alphabet

Teaching the Recognition of the Letter "Tt" and Its Sound

Objectives:

- To reinforce the recognition of the letter "Tt" and to introduce the sound that it makes.
- To strengthen listening skills and the ability to follow directions.
- To develop and improve communication skills.

Reproduce page 87 for your students.

Teacher Directed Activity:

1. Look at the letters at the top of the page. What are they called? (Tt)

2. Let's trace them with our fingers. Let's trace them in the air. Constantly reinforce starting positions and directions in which each letter flows.

3. Let's look at the pictures on the page. Point to each one and say its name.

tent, turkey, tie, toys

4. Using your green crayon, neatly color the tent. While the students are working discuss the word. What is a tent? When is a tent used? Have you ever slept in a tent? What did you use for a bed in a tent? Do you like to go camping?

5. Put your finger on the turkey. Using your orange crayon, draw a box around the turkey. Now color the turkey brown. Have you ever eaten turkey? Do you like it? When do we eat turkey? What does your mother put inside the turkey?

6. Using your red crayon, draw a circle around the tie. Color the tie blue. What is a tie? When does a man wear a tie? Where might a man wear a tie? Are all ties the same? How are they different?

7. Using your purple crayon, draw a wiggly line under the toys. Neatly color the toys using any crayons. What are toys? Who plays with toys? What can some toys do? What is your favorite toy?

8. Point to each picture and say its name after me.

tent, turkey, tie, toys

What sound do you hear at the beginning of each picture? (tih) When you make the sound at the beginning of tent, turkey, tie, and toys where is your tongue? (It is touching the part of my mouth above my front teeth.) I call this sound the clock ticking sound. It makes the sound a clock makes when it ticks. (tih - tih - tih)

Auditory Game:

- Listen to these words: **tap, ticket**
- Do they begin the same way? (Yes) What sound do you hear? (tih)
- Listen again. This time cover both ears with your hands if the words begin with the sound that "Tt" makes.
- Say the following groups of words and wait for a response.

a) time, table (Response)	b) door, doctor (No Response)	c) two, take (Response)
d) goat, gate (No Response)	e) tape, tan (Response)	f) jeep, jay (No Response)
g) turnip, tomato (Response)	h) lettuce, lemon (No Response)	i) tea, tooth (Response)

Conclusion:

- Review letters, formations, sounds, and rhymes that have been previously taught.

T t

tent

turkey

tie

toys

Teaching the Recognition of the Letter "Uu"

Objectives:

- To reinforce the recognition of the upper and lower case "Uu."
- To develop an awareness of the letter formation and how it is made.

Introduction:

Use a large alphabet card and the letter "Uu" cutouts. Pass out the letters to your students allowing them to trace around them with their fingers to note their shapes. Discuss the lines in each letter noting the straight lines and the curved lines.

Discussion:

1. Does anyone know the name for these letters? (Hold up the upper case "U" and the lower case "u.") Where do these letters live? (Point to the alphabet.) They live with 25 other letters in a big house called the alphabet. Who does the letter "Uu" live beside? (Tt) Does anyone have these letters in their names? Who has the big "U"? (Hold up the upper case "U.") Who has the little "u"? (Hold up the lower case "u.")

2. Discuss the shape of the upper case "U." What are the lines like in the big "U"? (straight, curved) How many lines are there? (one) Let's trace the big "U" with our fingers. Begin at the top of the first line and travel down to where it curves and travel along to where the curved line meets the straight line and travel up to the top. The big "U" is made in one movement. Make sure the students travel down the left side along the curved part and up the right side. Tell the students that the big "U" looks like a cup without a handle.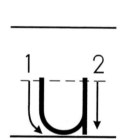

3. Discuss the shape of the lower case "u." Trace the shape of the lower case "u" to show its formation. Have your students notice that the small "u" is made in two steps not one. The first line is straight and then curves for a little way. The second line is straight and kisses the end of the curved line. Have your students trace the small "u" with their fingers. Start at the top of the first line and travel down the straight line to the curved line until it stops. Then put your finger on the top of the second line and travel down it and kiss the curved line. Practice making the upper and lower "Uu" in a variety of ways.

Student Activity: Alphabet Book

1. Reproduce page 89 with the letter "Uu" for your students.

2. Discuss the shapes of the letters. Encourage your students to color the letters in the same directions in which they traced them.

3. Have the students neatly color the picture of the "unicorn."

4. Discuss the words that say "unicorn" at the bottom of the page. Have your students identify the word "Unicorn" with the upper case "U" and then identify the word "unicorn" with the lower case "u."

5. Glue this page into the students' alphabet scrapbook.

6. Have the students color the room in which "Uu" lives on the **Alphabet House** page.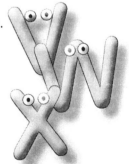

7. Recite this rhyme with your students.

> "Uu" is for unicorn,
> A horse so white.
> With a curly horn,
> What a magical sight!

8. Review letters, formations, sounds, and rhymes previously taught.

U u

Unicorn   unicorn

Teaching the Recognition of the Letter "Uu" and Its Sounds

Objectives:

- To reinforce the recognition of the letter "Uu" and to introduce the sounds that it makes.
- To strengthen listening skills and the ability to follow directions.
- To develop and improve communication skills.

Reproduce page 91 for your students.

Teacher Directed Activity:

1. Look at the letters at the top of the page. What are they called? (Uu)

2. Let's trace them with our fingers. Let's trace them in the air. Constantly reinforce starting positions and directions in which each letter flows.

3. Let's look at the pictures on the page. Point to each one and say its name.

   unicycle,   umbrella,   up,   ukulele

4. Using your green crayon put a wiggly line under the "unicycle." Now color it neatly. While the students are working, discuss the picture. What is a unicycle? Who might ride one? Where might you see one being ridden? How is a unicycle different from a bicycle? Do you think it would be easy to ride one?

5. Listen to the beginning of "unicycle." Exaggerate the long "u" sound at the beginning. Have them echo you. Tell your students the "Uu" is talking. What is it saying? (It is saying its own name?)

6. Point to the picture of the "umbrella." Neatly color the umbrella orange. Discuss the picture. When do you use an umbrella? Why do we use one? What can happen to your umbrella on a windy day?

7. Listen to the beginning of "umbrella." Exaggerate the sound the "u" makes. Have the students repeat the word. Have them place their hands under their jaws and say "umbrella." What happens at the beginning of umbrella? They will notice that their jaw drops and their mouths open wide. What sound do you hear at the beginning of umbrella? (uh)

8. Have your students locate the arrow going "up." Color the arrow going up red. Discuss the picture. Why do you think the arrow is going up? When you see an arrow pointing up in a store, what does that mean? When you look up what do you see?

9. Listen while I say the word "up." Exaggerate the "Uu" sound. The letter "Uu" is talking at the beginning of "up." Put your hand under your chin. Say the word "up." Can you hear it? What does it say? (uh) What does your chin do? (It drops.)

10. Put your finger on the "ukulele." Color it purple. Discuss the picture. What is a ukulele? How do you play one? What part makes the music? Can you think of another instrument that has strings?

11. Listen while I say the word "ukulele." Exaggerate the "Uu" sound. The letter "Uu" is talking at the beginning of "ukulele." Can you hear it? What does it say? (It says its own name.)

12. Let's look at the four pictures. Which pictures begin the same way? Listen while I say their names.

    a) umbrella, unicycle (No)   b) umbrella, up (Yes)
    c) up, unicycle (No)   d) unicycle, ukulele (Yes)

13. Explain to the students that the letter "Uu" can make two sounds. It can say its own name or its other sound (uh). Reinforce that the long "u" sound makes the mouth open a little while the short "u" sound makes the jaw drop and your mouth opens wide.

Conclusion:

- Review the letters, formations, sounds, and rhymes that have been previously taught.

U u

unicycle

umbrella

up

ukulele

Teaching the Recognition of the letter "Vv"

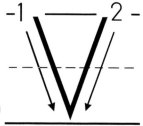

Objectives:
- To reinforce the recognition of the upper and lower case "Vv."
- To develop an awareness of the letter formation and how it is made.

Introduction:
Use a large alphabet card and the letter "Vv" cutouts. Pass out the letters to your students allowing them to trace around them with their fingers to note their shapes. Discuss the lines in each letter noting the straight lines and where they meet.

Discussion:
1. Does anyone know the name for these letters? (Hold up the upper case "V" and the lower case "v.") Where do these letters live? (Point to the alphabet.) They live with 25 other letters in a big house called the alphabet. Who does the letter "Vv" live beside. (Uu) Does any one have these letters in their names? Who has the big "V"? (Hold up the upper case "V.") Who has the little "v"? (Hold up the lower case "v.")

2. Discuss the shape of the upper case "V." What are the lines like in the big "V"? (straight, slanted lines) How many lines are there? (two) Let's trace the big "V" with our fingers. Begin at the top of the first line and travel down it to the point. Take your fingers away and place them at the top of the second line. Now travel down it to the point. Does this letter remind you of a part of other letters that we have discussed. (the middle of the letter "M", the end of "N" and an upside down "A.") Let's practice making the big "V" in the air, on a table, and on the palm of your hand.

3. Discuss the shape of the lower case "v." Trace the lower case "v" to show its formation. What do you notice about the big "V" and the little "v"? (They are made exactly the same way and look the same.) How are they different? (The big "V" is made bigger than the little "v.") Let's trace both letters in the air, on a table, and on the palms of our hands. Make sure the students make two downward strokes.

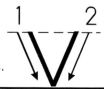

Student Activity: Alphabet Book
1. Reproduce page 93 with the letter "Vv" for your students.
2. Discuss the shapes of the letters. Encourage your students to color the letters in the same direction in which they traced them.
3. Have the students neatly color the "valentine."
4. Discuss the words that say "valentine" at the bottom of the page. Have your students identify the word "Valentine" with the upper case "V" and then identify the word "valentine" with the lower case "v."
5. Glue this page into the students' alphabet scrapbooks.
6. Have the students color the room in which "Vv" lives on the **Alphabet House** page.
7. Recite this rhyme with your students.

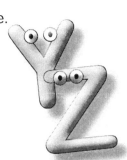

> "Vv" is for valentine,
> A card that says.
> Will you be mine?
> On Valentine's Day.

8. Review letters, formations, sounds, and rhymes previously taught.

V v

Valentine   valentine

Teaching the Recognition of the Letter "Vv" and Its Sound

Objectives:

- To reinforce the recognition of the letter "Vv" and to introduce the sound that it makes.
- To strengthen listening skills and the ability to follow directions.
- To develop and improve communication skills.

Reproduce page 95 for your students.

Teacher Directed Activity:

1. Look at the letters at the top of the page. What are they called? (Vv)

2. Let's trace them with our fingers. Let's trace them in the air. Constantly reinforce starting positions and directions in which each letter flows.

3. Let's look at the pictures on the page. Point to each one and say its name.

    vegetables,   violin,   vest,   vine

4. Using your green crayon, circle the picture of the vegetables. Now neatly color them. Discuss the picture with your students. What are vegetables? Name the vegetables in the picture. Do you like to eat vegetables? Which vegetable is your favorite? Which one is your least favorite?

5. Above the picture of the violin, make a big blue dot. Color the violin brown. Discuss the picture. What is a violin? What happens when you play one? What is used to play a violin? From where does the music come? Do you know another name for a violin?

6. Under the picture of the vest, draw a red line. Now color the vest yellow. What is a vest? When do you wear a vest? How is a vest different from a coat or jacket?

7. Put a green circle around the picture of the vine. Color the vine green. Discuss the picture. What is a vine? What kind of fruit grows on a vine? Where do vines like to grow?

8. Point to each picture and say its name after me.

    vegetables,   violin,   vest,   vine

What sound do you hear at the beginning of each picture? (vuh) When you make the sound at the beginning of vegetables, violin, vest, and vine where are your teeth? (They are resting on my bottom lip.) When you make the "vuh" sound, what do you feel on your bottom lip? (Air and movement that tickles my bottom lip.) I call this sound the lip tickling sound. When you make the "vuh" sound it makes air that tickles your bottom lip.

Auditory Game:

- Listen to these words: **vinegar, vase**
- Do they begin the same way? (Yes) What sound do you hear? (vuh)
- Listen again. This time close your eyes if the word begins with the sound that "Vv" makes.
- Say the following groups of words and wait for a response.

    a) vine, vet (Response)   b) finger, father (No Response)   c) velvet, violin (Response)
    d) pumpkin, door (No Response)   e) goat, gas (No Response)   f) view, voice (Response)
    g) vegetables, vacuum (Response) h) cookie, nose (No Response)   i) valentine, vine (Response)

Conclusion:

- Review the letters, formations, sounds, and rhymes previously taught.

V v

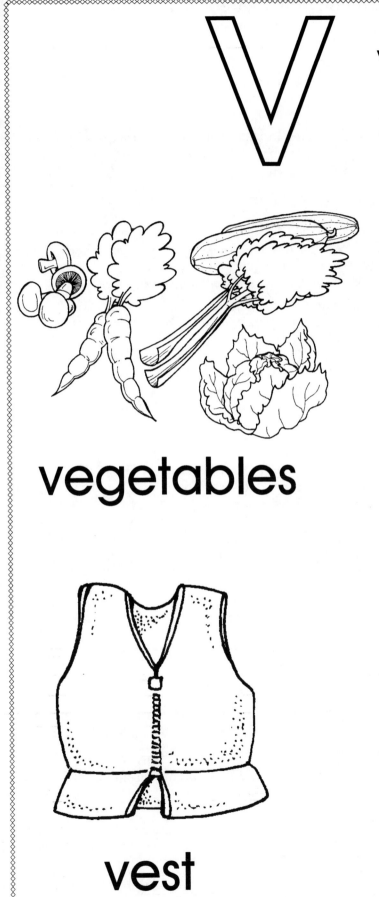

vegetables

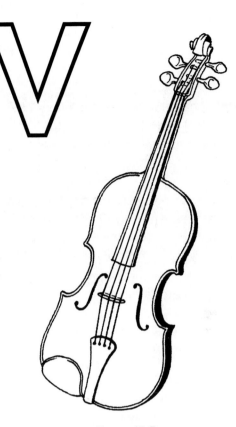

violin

vest

vine

 OTM-18103 • SSR1-103 The Alphabet

Teaching the Recognition of the letter "Ww"

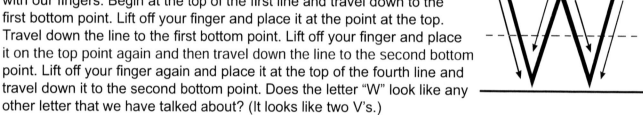

Objectives:

- To reinforce the recognition of the upper and lower case "Ww."
- To develop an awareness of the letter formation and how it is made.

Introduction:

Use a large alphabet card and the letter "Ww" cutouts. Pass out the letters to your students allowing them to trace around them with their fingers to note their shapes. Discuss the lines in each letter noting the straight, slanted lines and the points.

Discussion:

1. Does anyone know the name for these letters? (Hold up the upper case "W" and the lower case "w.") Where do these letters live? (Point to the alphabet.) They live with 25 other letters in a big house called the alphabet. Who does the "Ww" live beside? (Vv) Does anyone have these letters in their names? Who has the big "W"? (Hold up the upper case "W".) Who has the little "w"? (Hold up the lower case "w.")

2. Discuss the shape of the upper case "W." (straight, slanted lines, three points) How many lines are in the big "W"? (four) Let's trace the big "W" with our fingers. Begin at the top of the first line and travel down to the first bottom point. Lift off your finger and place it at the point at the top. Travel down the line to the first bottom point. Lift off your finger and place it on the top point again and then travel down the line to the second bottom point. Lift off your finger again and place it at the top of the fourth line and travel down it to the second bottom point. Does the letter "W" look like any other letter that we have talked about? (It looks like two V's.)

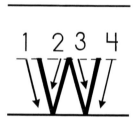

3. Discuss the shape of the lower case "w." Trace the lower case "w" to show its formation. Have your students notice that the upper and lower case "Ww" are made exactly the same way. How are the big "W" and the little "w" different? (One is smaller.) Have them note that the little letter "w" is also made of two little v's as well. Practice making the upper and lower case "Ww" in the air, on a table, and on the palm of your hand. Make sure the students move from left to right and from top to bottom while forming the letters.

Student Activity: Alphabet Book

1. Reproduce page 97 with the letter "Ww" for your students.

2. Discuss the shapes of the letters. Encourage your students to color the letters in the same directions in which they traced them.

3. Have the students neatly color the picture of the "walrus."

4. Discuss the words that say "walrus" at the bottom of the page. Have the students identify the word "Walrus" with the upper case "W" and then identify the word "walrus" with the lower case "w."

5. Glue this page into the students' alphabet scrapbooks.

6. Have the students color the room in which the letter "Ww" lives on the **Alphabet House** page.

7. Recite this rhyme with your students.

> "Ww" is for walrus,
> Who lives on the ice.
> Waiting for a fish,
> Fat and nice.

8. Review letters, formations, sounds, and rhymes previously taught.

W w

Walrus   walrus

OTM-18103 • SSR1-103 The Alphabet

Teaching the Recognition of the Letter "Ww" and Its Sound

Objectives:

- To reinforce the recognition of the letter "Ww" and to introduce the sound that it makes.
- To strengthen listening skills and the ability to follow directions.
- To develop and improve communication skills.

Reproduce page 99 for your students.

Teacher Directed Activity:

1. Look at the letters at the top of the page. What are they called? (Ww)

2. Let's trace them with our fingers. Let's trace them in the air. Constantly reinforce starting positions and the directions in which each letter flows.

3. Let's look at the pictures on the page. Point to each one and say its name.

wall,   well,   wind,   witch

4. Point to the picture of the wall. Using your red crayon, neatly color the brick wall. While your students are working, discuss the picture. What is a wall? What is a wall used for? What kinds of things are used to make a wall? Why did people build walls around their castles? Can you think of a nursery rhyme character who sat on a wall and then fell off?

5. Point to the well. Draw a blue circle around the well. Neatly color the well any way that you like. Discuss the picture. What would you find in a well? How do you get water out of a well? What nursery rhyme characters went up to a well to get some water? Do people still use wells? Where?

6. Point to the picture of the wind blowing. Draw two blue lines under the picture of the wind. Now neatly color the picture. Discuss the picture. What does the wind do to things? What good things does the wind do? What are the bad things that the wind does? When is the wind the coldest? When is the wind the warmest?

7. Point to the witch. Neatly color the make-believe witch. Discuss the picture. What is a make-believe witch? When would we see one? Where does a make-believe witch live? What is a make-believe witch able to do with her broom? Can you think of a story that has a make-believe witch in it?

8. Point to each picture and say its name after me.

wall,   well,   wind,   witch

What sound do you hear at the beginning of each picture? (wuh) Put your hand in front of your mouth and say each word again. What do you feel on your hand at the beginning of each word? (air) The letter "Ww" has a windy sound. I call the letter "Ww" the windy sound.

Auditory Game:

- Listen to these words: **wagon, water**
- Do they begin the same way? (Yes) What sound do you hear? (wuh)
- Listen again. This time put your hands at your sides like a soldier if the words begin with the sound that "Ww" makes.
- Say the following groups of words and wait for a response.

a) William, Wayne (Response)	b) road, ride (No Response)	c) wiggle, worm (Response)
d) sandwich, salad (No Response)	e) wash, wish (Response)	f) van, violet (No Response)
g) wave, walk (Response)	h) window, warm (Response)	i) tent, table (No Response)

Conclusion:

- Review letters, formations, sounds, and rhymes that have been previously taught.

W w

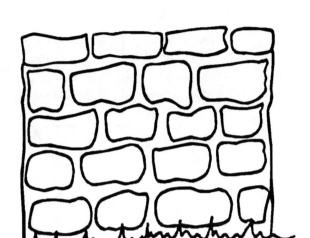

wall

well

wind

witch

Teaching the Recognition of the Letter "Xx"

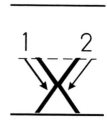

Objectives:

- To reinforce the recognition of the upper and lower case "Xx".
- To develop an awareness of the letter formation and how it is made.

Introduction:

Use a large alphabet card and the letter "Xx" cutouts. Pass out the letters to your students allowing them to trace around them with their fingers to note their shapes. Discuss the lines in each letter noting the straight, slanted lines.

Discussion:

1. Does anyone know the name for these letters? (Hold up the upper case "X" and the lower case "x.") Where do these letters live? (Point to the alphabet.) They live with 25 other letters in a big house called the alphabet. Who does the letter "Xx" live beside? (Ww) Does anyone have these letters in their names? Who has the big "X"? (Hold up the upper case "X.") Who has the little "x"? (Hold up the lower case "x.")

2. Discuss the shape of the upper case "X." What are the lines like in the big "X." (straight, slanted, crossed in the middle) How many lines are there? (two) Let's trace the upper case "X" with our fingers. Begin at the top of the first slanted line and travel all the way to the bottom. Now put your finger at the top of the second slanted line and travel to the bottom. Practice making the upper case "X" in a variety of ways.

3. Discuss the shape of the lower case "x." Trace the lower case "x" to show its formation. Have your students notice that the upper and lower case "Xx" look exactly the same and are made the same way. How are the big "X" and the little "x" different? (One is smaller.) Practice making the upper and lower case "Xx" in the air, on a table, and on the palms of their hands. Make sure the students move from left to right and from top to bottom while forming the letters.

Student Activity: Alphabet Book

1. Reproduce page 101 with the letter "Xx" for your students.

2. Discuss the shapes of the letters. Encourage your students to color the letters in the same directions in which they traced them.

3. Have the students neatly color the picture of the "xylophone."

4. Discuss the words that say "xylophone" at the bottom of the page. Have your students identify the word "Xylophone" with the upper case "X" and then identify the word "xylophone' with the lower case "x."

5. Glue this page into the students' alphabet scrapbooks.

6. Have the students color the room in which the letter "Xx" lives on the **Alphabet House** page.

7. Recite this rhyme with your students.

> Xx is for xylophone,
> Something we can play.
> To make pretty music,
> On a sunny day.

8. Review letters, formations, sounds, and rhymes previously taught.

Xylophone xylophone

Teaching the Recognition of the Letter "Xx" and Its Sound

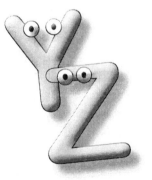

Objectives:

- To reinforce the recognition of the letter "Xx" and to introduce the sound that it makes.
- To strengthen listening skills and the ability to follow directions.
- To develop and improve communication skills.

Reproduce page 103 for your students.

Teacher Directed Activity:

1. Look at the letters at the top of the page. What are they called? (Xx)

2. Let's trace them with our fingers. Let's trace them in the air. Constantly reinforce starting positions and directions in which each letter flows.

3. Let's look at the pictures on the page. Point to each one and say its name.

x-ray,   xylophone,   Xmas

4. Using your pencil, draw a box around the x-ray. Color the picture neatly. While the students are working discuss the picture. What is a x-ray? Where would you go to have a x-ray done? What does a x-ray show you? Have you ever had a x-ray?

5. Using your pencil, circle the xylophone. Color the picture neatly. What is a xylophone? What do you use to play one? Where would you see one being played? Have you ever played a xylophone?

6. Color the picture of Xmas neatly. Sometimes Christmas is called Xmas. When does Xmas take place? Who comes during Xmas? What do you get at Xmas?

7. Point to each picture and say its name after me.

x-ray,   xylophone,   Xmas

What sound do you hear at the beginning of each picture? (x-s) What sound does it remind you of? (Ss) I call this sound the kissing sound because people sign kisses using an "Xx" (x-s-s-s)

Auditory Game:

- Listen to this word: **extra**
- Does it have the sound that "Xx" makes? (Yes)
- Listen again. If the word that I say has the sound that "Xx" makes in it, stand up. If it doesn't remain seated.

a) box (Response)   b) oxygen (Response)   c) bottle (No Response)   d) extra (Response)
e) tax (Response)   f) examine (Response   g) table (No Response)   h) fox (Response)
i) food (No Response)

Conclusion:

- Review the letters, formations, sounds, and rhymes that have been previously taught.

X x

x-ray

xylophone

Xmas

OTM-18103 • SSR1-103 The Alphabet

Teaching the Recognition of the Letter "Yy"

Objectives:

- To reinforce the recognition of the upper and lower case "Yy."
- To develop an awareness of the letter formation and how it is made.

Introduction:

Use a large alphabet card and the letter "Yy" cutouts. Pass out the letters to your students. Allowing them to trace around them with their fingers to note their shapes. Discuss the lines in each letter noting the straight lines.

Discussion:

1. Does anyone know the name for these letters. (Hold up the upper case "Y" and the lower case "y.") Where do these letters live? (Point to the alphabet.) They live with 25 other letters in a big house called the alphabet. Who does the letter "Yy" live beside? (Xx) Does anyone have these letters in their names? Who has the big "Y"? (Hold up the upper case "Y.") Who has the little "y"? (Hold up the lower case "y.")

2. Discuss the shape of the upper case "Y." What are the lines like in the big "Y"? (straight, slanted, short) How many lines are there in the big "Y"? (three) Let's trace the big "Y" with our fingers. Begin at the top of the first line and travel down to the top of the third line. Now start at the top of the second line and travel down to the top of the third line? What letter have you just made? (the letter "v") Now make the third line. Start at the point of the "v" and travel down to the bottom. This line is holding up the letter "V." Now you have made the big letter "Y." Let's make it in the air, on a table, and on the palm of your hand.

3. Discuss the shape of the lower case "y." Trace the lower case "y" to show its formation. Have the students notice that the lower case "y" is similar to the upper case "Y" but it is only made of two lines. One line is short and one line is long. Have them make the short line first and then make the longer line next. Remind them that there are two movements. Tell them that the little "y" is also a tail letter. Review other tail letters such as the g, j, p, and q.

Student Activity: Alphabet Book

1. Reproduce page 105 with the letter "Yy" for your students.

2. Discuss the shapes of the letters. Encourage your students to color the letters in the same directions in which they traced them.

3. Have the students neatly color the picture of the "yard."

4. Discuss the words that say "yard" at the bottom of the page. Have your students identify the word "Yard" with the upper case "Y" and then identify the word "yard" with the lower case "y."

5. Glue this page into the students' alphabet scrapbooks.

6. Have the students color the room in which the letter "Yy" lives on the **Alphabet House** page.

7. Recite this rhyme with your students.

> "Yy" is for my yard,
> Where I like to play.
> On my swing,
> On a bright, sunny day.

8. Review letters, formations, sounds, and rhymes previously taught.

Yard yard

Teaching the Recognition of the Letter "Yy" and Its Sound

Objectives:

- To reinforce the recognition of the letter "Yy" and to introduce the sound that it makes.
- To strengthen listening skills and the ability to follow directions.
- To develop and improve communication skills.

Reproduce page 107 for your students.

Teacher Directed Activity:

1. Look at the letters at the top of the page. What are they called? (Yy)

2. Let's trace them with our fingers. Let's trace them in the air. Constantly reinforce starting positions and directions in which each letter flows.

3. Let's look at the pictures on the page. Point to each one and say its name.

yak,   yarn,   yoyo,   yawn

4. Put your finger on the "yak." Color it brown. While the students are working, discuss the picture. What is a yak? Where does a yak live? Have you ever seen one? What does the yak have on its head? What kind of fur or hair does a yak have?

5. Put your finger on the ball of "yarn." Color the yarn red. What is yarn? What is yarn used for? What is another name for yarn? What farm animal gives us the material to make yarn?

6. Put your finger on the "yoyo." Neatly color it orange. What is a yoyo? What can you do with a yoyo? What is a yoyo made of? What does the yoyo travel up and down on? Have you ever played with a yoyo?

7. Circle the picture of the man yawning. Color the man neatly. Why do you think the man is yawning? When do you yawn? What should you do while you are yawning?

8. Point to the picture and say its name after me.

yak,   yarn,   yoyo,   yawn

What sound do you hear at the beginning of each picture? (yuh) When you make the sound at the beginning of yak, yarn, yoyo, and yawn what does your jaw do? (It drops open.) I call this sound the lazy way to say the word yes sound. (Yuh)

Auditory Game:

- Listen to these words: **yummy, yesterday**
- Do they begin the same way? (Yes) What sound do you hear? (yuh)
- Listen again. This time put your hands on your ears if the words begin with the sound that "Yy" makes.
- Say the following groups of words and wait for a response.

a) yellow, yank (Response)	b) goat, gun (No Response)	c) year, yet (Response)
d) pig, dog (No Response)	e) yolk, yours (Response)	f) barn, lake (No Response)
g) your, yes (Response)	h) ribbon, stairs (No Response)	i) yam, yacht (Response)

Conclusion:

- Review the letters, formations, sounds, and rhymes that have been previously taught.

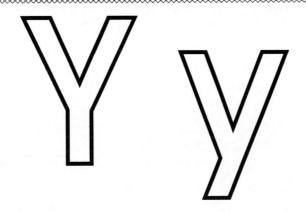

yak

yarn

yoyo

yawn

 OTM-18103 • SSR1-103 The Alphabet

Teaching the Recognition of the Letter "Zz"

Objectives:

- To reinforce the recognition of the upper and lower case "Zz."
- To develop an awareness of the letter formation and how it is made.

Introduction:

Use a large alphabet card and the letter "Zz" cutouts. Pass out the letters to your students allowing them to trace around them with their fingers to note their shapes. Discuss the lines in each letter.

Discussion:

1. Does anyone know the name for these letters? (Hold up the upper case "Z" and the lower case "z.") Where do these letters live? (Point to the alphabet.) They live with 25 other letters in a big house called the alphabet. Who does the letter "Zz" live beside? (Yy) Does anyone have these letters in their names? Who has the big "Z"? (Hold up the upper case "Z.") Who has the little "z"? (Hold up the lower case "z.")

2. Discuss the shape of the upper case "Z." What are the lines like in the big "Z"? (straight, slanted) How many lines are there in the big "Z"? (three) Let's trace the big "Z" with our fingers. Begin at the end of the first line and travel along it until you reach the end. Take your finger away. Now put your finger on the end of slanted line and travel down it to the bottom. Take your finger away. Now put your finger on the beginning of the last line at the bottom and travel along it to the end.

3. Discuss the shape of the lower case "z." Trace the lower case "z" to show its formation. Have your students notice that the lower case "z" looks exactly like the upper case "Z" and it is made exactly the same way only smaller. Practice making the lower case "z" in various ways.

Student Activity: Alphabet Book

1. Reproduce page 109 with the letter "Zz" for your students.

2. Discuss the shapes of the letters. Encourage the students to color the letters in the same directions in which they traced them.

3. Have the students neatly color the picture of the "zebra."

4. Discuss the words that say "zebra" at the bottom of the page. Have your students identify the word "Zebra" with the upper case "Z" and then identify the word "zebra" with the lower case "z."

5. Glue this page into the students' alphabet scrapbooks.

6. Have the students color the room in which the letter "Zz" lives on the Alphabet House page.

7. Recite this rhyme with your students.

> "Zz" is for zebra,
> A funny sight.
> A little striped horse,
> All black and white.

8. Review all the letters in the students' alphabet book. Try to review all the rhymes as well. Send the book home with the students to show their parents.

Zebra zebra

Teaching the Recognition of the Letter Zz and Its Sound

Objectives:

- To reinforce the recognition of the letter "Zz" and to introduce the sound that it makes.
- To strengthen listening skills and the ability to follow directions.
- To develop and improve communication skills.

Reproduce page 111 for your students.

Teacher Directed Activity:

1. Look at the letters at the top of the page. What are they called? (Zz)

2. Let's trace them with our fingers. Let's trace them in the air. Constantly reinforce starting positions and directions in which each letter flows.

3. Let's look at the pictures on the page. Point to each one and say its name.

zipper,   zoo,   zero,   zig-zag

4. Using your blue crayon, circle the zipper. While the students are working, discuss the picture. What is a zipper? What do we use a zipper for? In what type of clothing would you find a zipper? In what other things is a zipper used.

5. Color the picture of the zoo neatly. What is a zoo? What would you find at a zoo? Can you name some zoo animals? Have you ever been to a zoo? What is your favorite zoo animal?

6. Color the zero blue. What is a zero? What does it mean if the temperature outside is at zero? If you have zero money, how much money do you have?

7. Draw a line under the zig-zag line. Color the zig-zag line yellow. Have you ever seen a zig-zag line in the sky when there is a storm? What makes the zig-zag line?

8. Point to each picture and say its name after me.

zipper,   zoo,   zero,   zig-zag

What sound do you hear at the beginning of each picture? (z-z-z) When you make the sound at the beginning of zipper, zoo, zero, and zig-zag where is your tongue? (Behind my teeth) Is your mouth open or closed? (closed) I call this sound the bee buzzing sound. It is the same sound a bee makes when it is buzzing around a flower in the garden.

Auditory Game:

- Listen to these words: **Zack, Zoey**
- Do they begin the same way? (Yes) What sound do you hear? (z-z-z)
- Listen again. This time I want you to make the bee buzzing sound if the words begin with the sound the "Zz" makes.
- Say the following words and wait for a response.

  a) sun, star (No Response)   b) zoom, zero (Response)   c) zinc, zap (Response)
  d) car, cookie (No Response)   e) zipper, zero (Response)   f) zucchini, zip (Response)
  g) fawn, fellow (No Response)   h) top, ticket (No Response) i) zebra, zoo (Response)

Conclusions:

- Review the letters, formations, sounds, and rhymes previously taught.

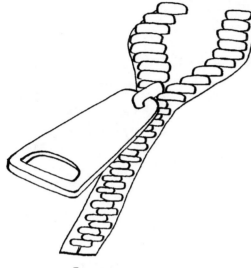

zipper

zoo

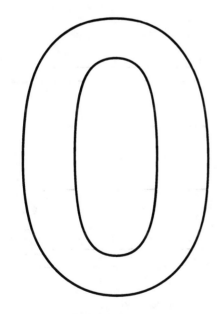

zero

zig-zag

OTM-18103 • SSR1-103 The Alphabet

Match the letters on the mittens.

r s u u a z

A N R Z U S

Match the letters on the balls.

t m b e c p

C E M P Q T

OTM-18103 • SSR1-103 The Alphabet

Match the letters on the cookies

k   P   h   v   I   i

H   L   I   P   V   K

Match the letters on the apples.

b   o   p   Y   f   j

Y   B   F   J   O   D

Match the letters on the blocks.

x	W
n	M
m	X
w	F
b	B
f	N

Circle the letters in the big box that look like the letter in the little box.

A	V	A	M	A	W	A	C	A
B	D	P	B	O	B	G	C	B
C	G	Q	C	D	C	P	V	E
D	C	D	G	D	H	D	J	I
E	E	F	Z	E	F	T	R	E
F	L	F	T	F	O	R	R	W

Circle the letters in the big box that look the same as the one in the little box.

S	T	S	M	R	S	C	D	R
T	I	T	J	T	U	K	T	N
U	N	U	F	D	U	R	Y	U
V	W	V	A	V	W	V	N	M
W	M	A	W	N	W	H	W	
X	Y	X	J	X	T	Z	X	N

Circle the letters in the big box that look the same as the one in the little box.

Z	A	Z	B	Z	H	N	Z	X
Y	X	V	Y	Z	L	Y	T	Y
R	B	R	P	R	G	R	D	E
W	M	N	W	A	W	Y	W	X
V	Y	V	W	M	V	N	V	T
N	M	N	W	N	V	T	N	

OTM-18103 • SSR1-103 The Alphabet

Circle the letters in the big box that look the same as the one in the litte box.

G	C G R Q G H D G
H	M N H R H L H T
I	T I L I J I Z V
J	G J P S J K N J
K	K H M K R X K P
L	I L L T F L N L

Circle the letters in the big box that look the same as the one in the little box.

M	N M O W M F M S
N	W C N B N O N Y
O	O Q R C O J K O
P	R P D P B P Q P
Q	O C Q R Q D Q N
R	P B R G R W R N

Circle the letters in the big box that look like the one in the little box.

a	o	a	b	a	c	d	a	p
b	d	a	q	b	d	b	p	b
c	o	c	e	c	b	d	c	n
d	d	b	c	p	d	a	d	m
e	c	e	o	x	e	d	g	e
f	l	i	f	j	f	t	f	k
g	p	b	g	j	d	g	a	h

Circle the letters in the big box that look like the one in the little box.

h	l	t	h	b	d	h	k	h
i	j	l	i	m	i	t	i	x
j	g	p	j	q	j	y	j	u
k	b	k	e	i	k	d	f	k
l	i	k	d	l	b	l	f	l
m	n	u	m	w	v	m	r	m
n	m	o	h	n	k	f	n	j

Circle the letters in the big box that look the same as the one in the little box.

o	o	p	q	o	b	o	d	l
p	q	p	b	p	d	o	p	g
q	g	p	q	d	b	q	o	q
r	n	m	r	s	t	r	h	r
s	c	m	s	t	s	z	s	x
t	l	h	t	b	t	d	t	f
u	n	r	u	c	u	o	s	v

Circle the letters in the big box that look the same as the one in the little box.

v	w	y	v	n	o	v	x	v
w	m	w	v	w	y	x	z	w
x	y	z	x	t	v	x	u	x
y	p	y	g	y	q	j	y	f
z	n	z	x	z	y	t	z	v
u	n	r	u	c	o	s	u	u
q	p	q	g	j	q	y	q	d

Some of Andy Alligator's eggs are hatching.
His eggs have the letter Aa.
Color his eggs blue.

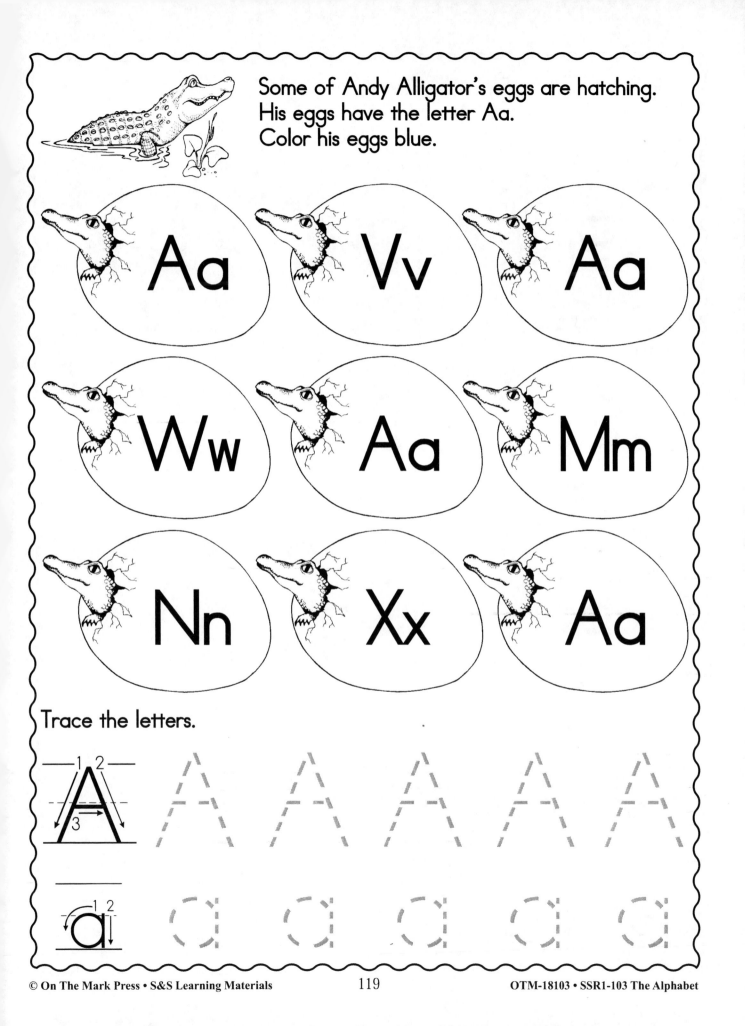

Aa   Vv   Aa

Ww   Aa   Mm

Nn   Xx   Aa

Trace the letters.

A A A A A A

a a a a a a

Billy Bee is looking for his beehives.
His beehives have the letter Bb.
Color his beehives yellow.

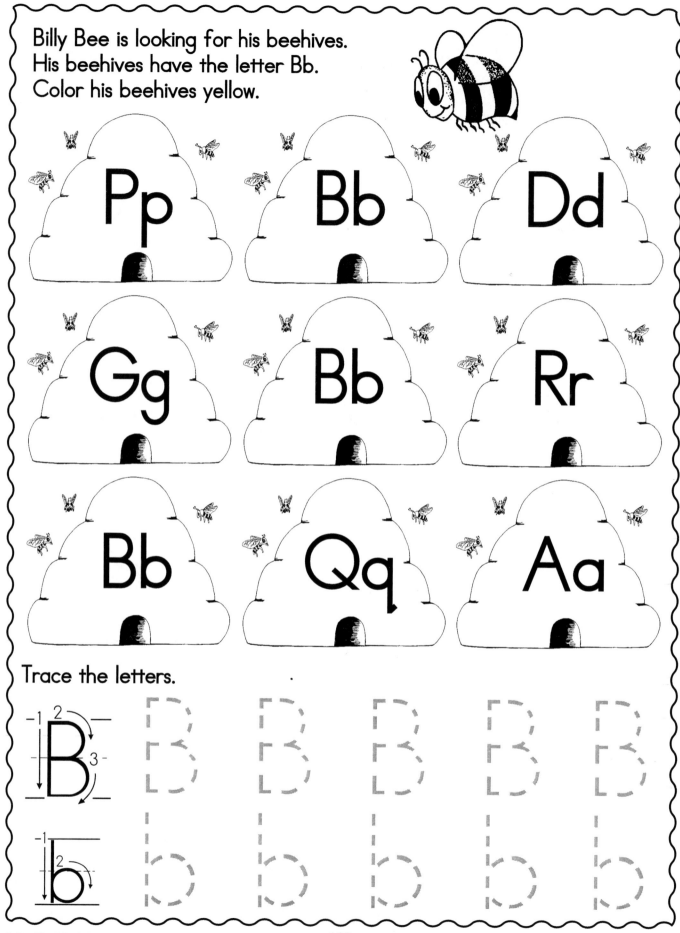

Pp   Bb   Dd

Gg   Bb   Rr

Bb   Qq   Aa

Trace the letters.

Carl Clown is looking for his balloons.
His balloons have the letter Cc.
Color his balloons red.

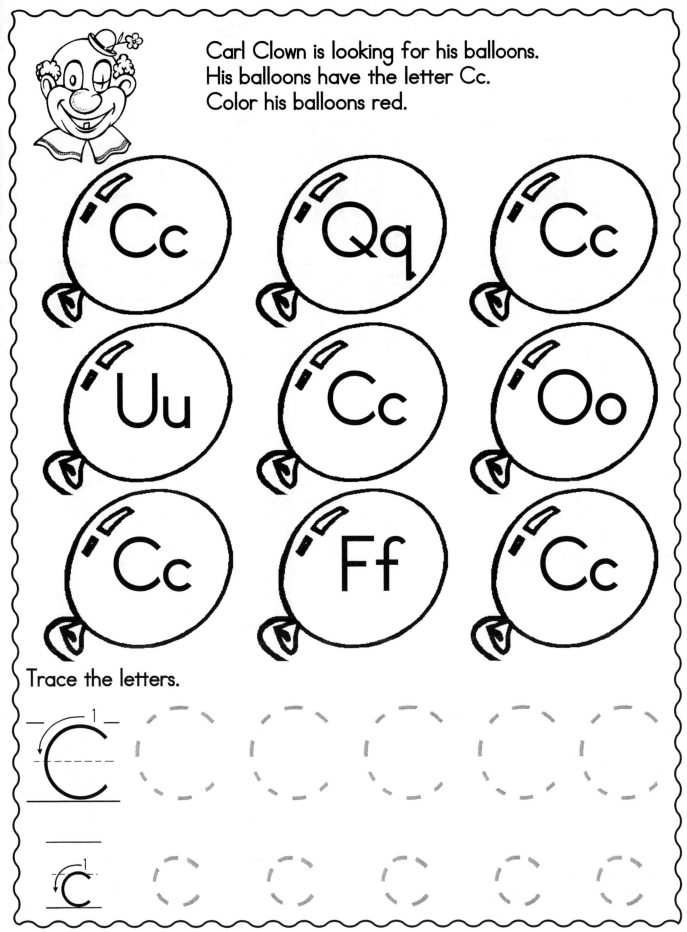

Cc   Qq   Cc

Uu   Cc   Oo

Cc   Ff   Cc

Trace the letters.

Dilly Dinosaur laid some dinosaur eggs.
His eggs have the letter Dd.
Color his eggs brown.

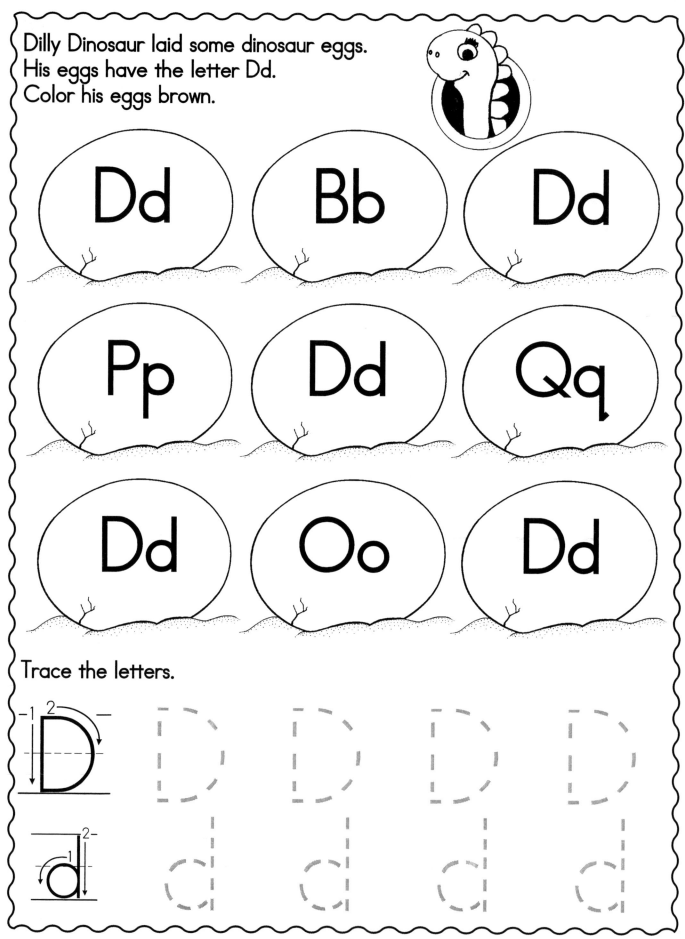

Trace the letters.

Ernie Elf is looking for his pots of gold.
His pots have the letter Ee.
Color his pots green.

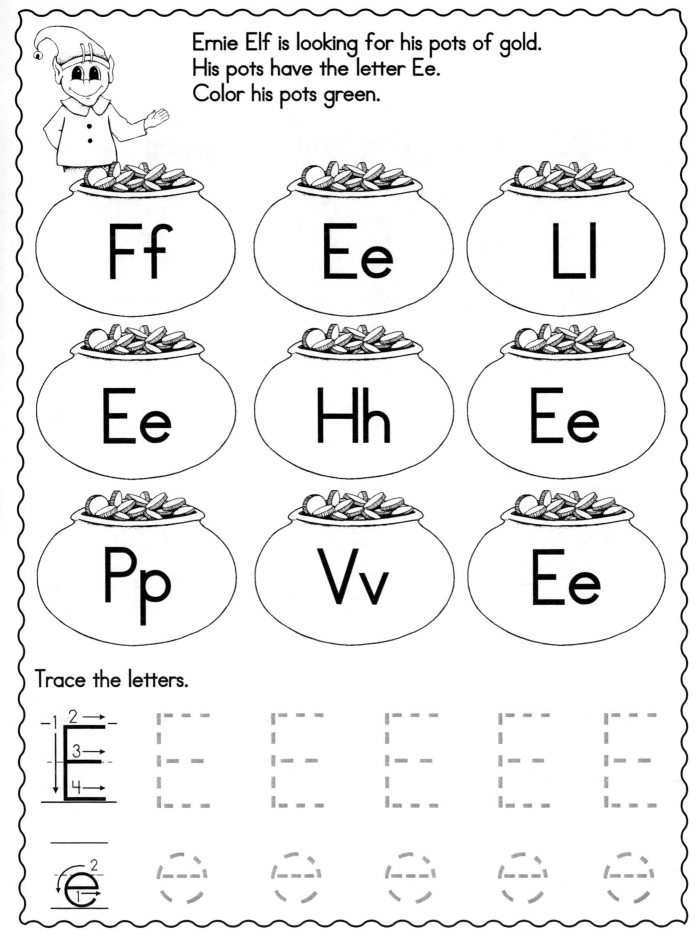

Ff   Ee   Ll

Ee   Hh   Ee

Pp   Vv   Ee

Trace the letters.

E E E E E E

e

Fanny Fairy likes to sprinkle fairy dust.
Her bags of fairy dust have the letter Ff.
Color her bags of fairy dust purple.

Trace the letters.

Gus Goldfish is looking for his bowls.
His bowls have the letter Gg.
Color his bowls blue.

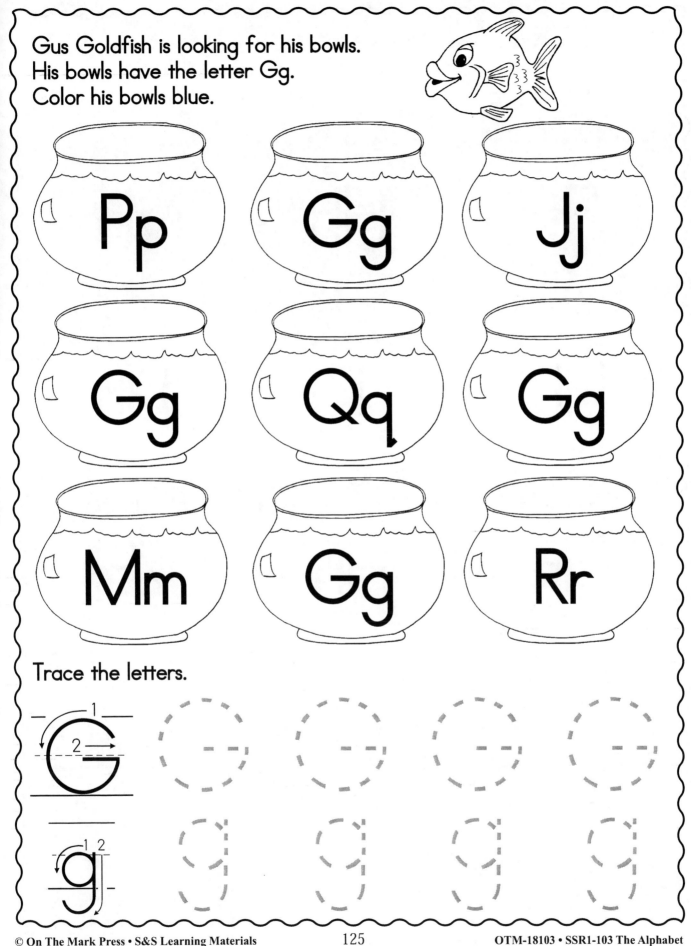

Pp Gg Jj

Gg Qq Gg

Mm Gg Rr

Trace the letters.

G

g

Harry Horse lives in several barns.
He lives in the barns that have the letter Hh.
Color his barns green.

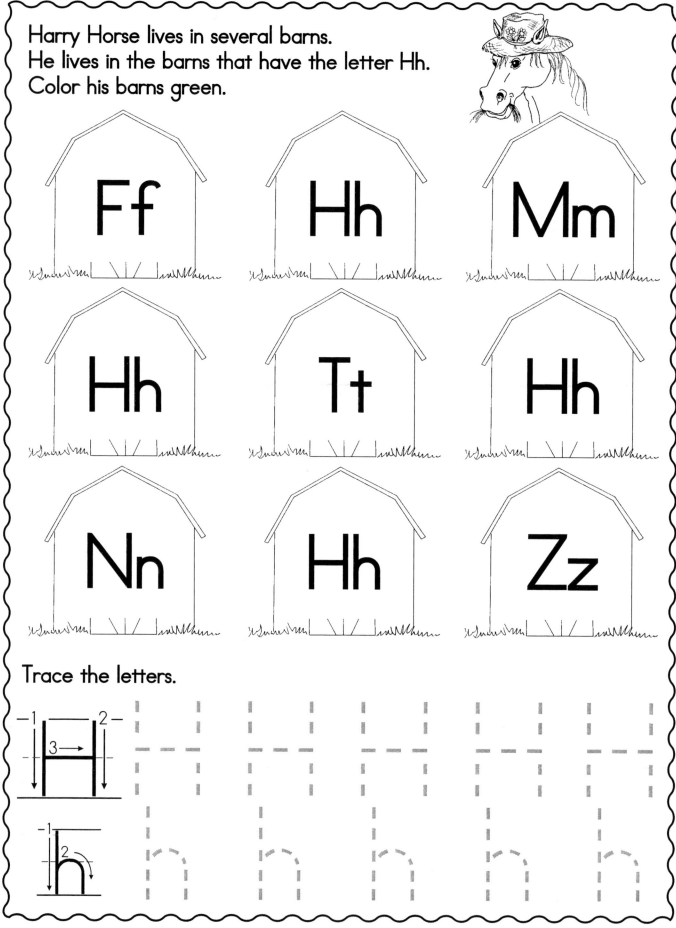

F f   H h   M m

H h   T t   H h

N n   H h   Z z

Trace the letters.

This Inuit boy built many igloos.
His igloos have the letter Ii.
Color his igloos different colors.

Ii   Ll   Tt

Hh   Ii   Jj

Ii   Kk   Ii

Trace the letters.

Jill is making some jack-o-lanterns with some pumpkins
Her pumpkins that she is using have the letter Jj.
Color Jill's pumpkin's orange.

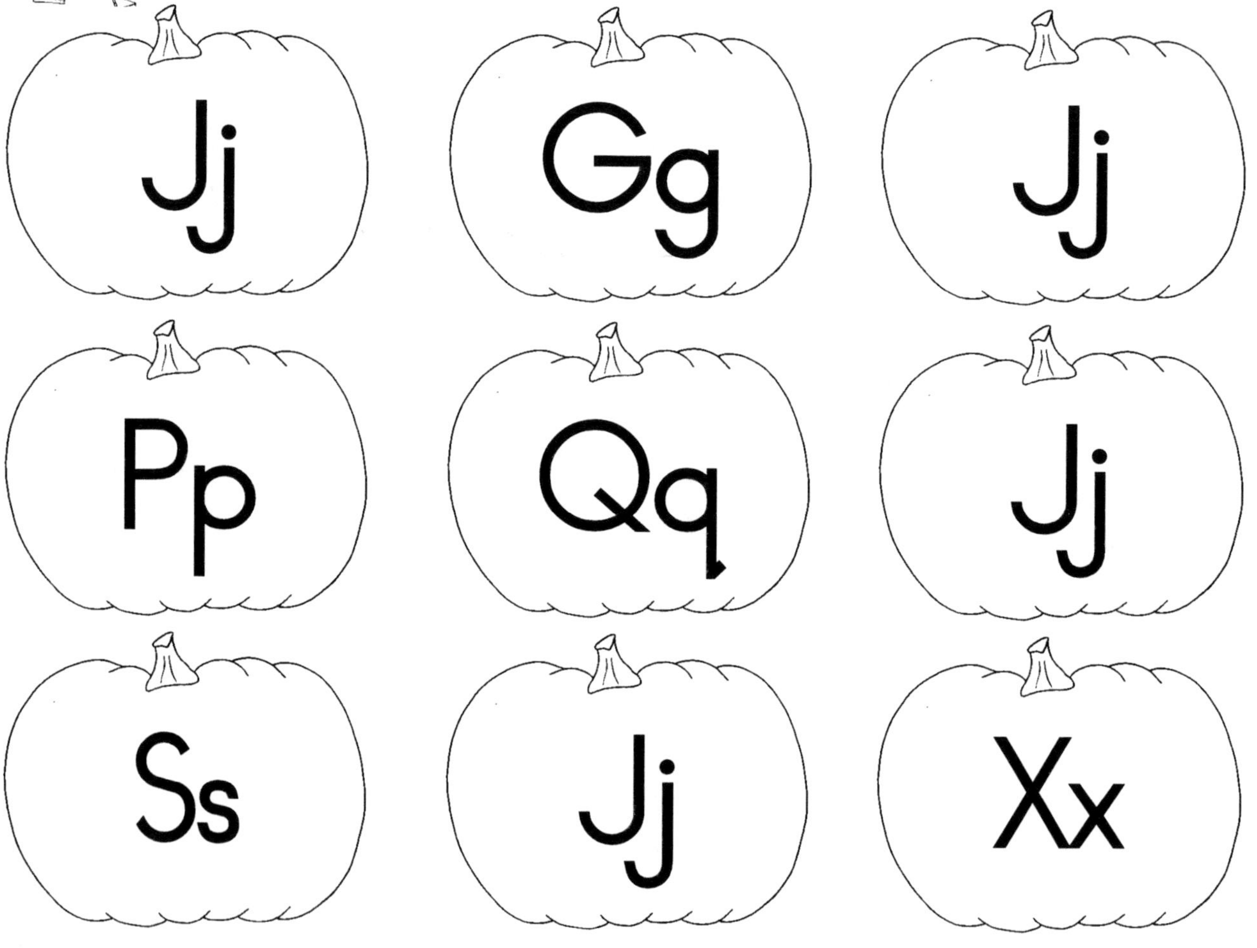

Jj   Gg   Jj

Pp   Qq   Jj

Ss   Jj   Xx

Trace the letters.

J

j

Kitty Kitten likes to play with balls of wool.
The balls that she plays with have the letter Kk.
Color the balls that belong to Kitty red.

Trace the letters.

Lucy loves to lick lollipops.
The lollipops that Lucy likes have the letter Ll.
Color the lollipops that Lucy likes yellow.

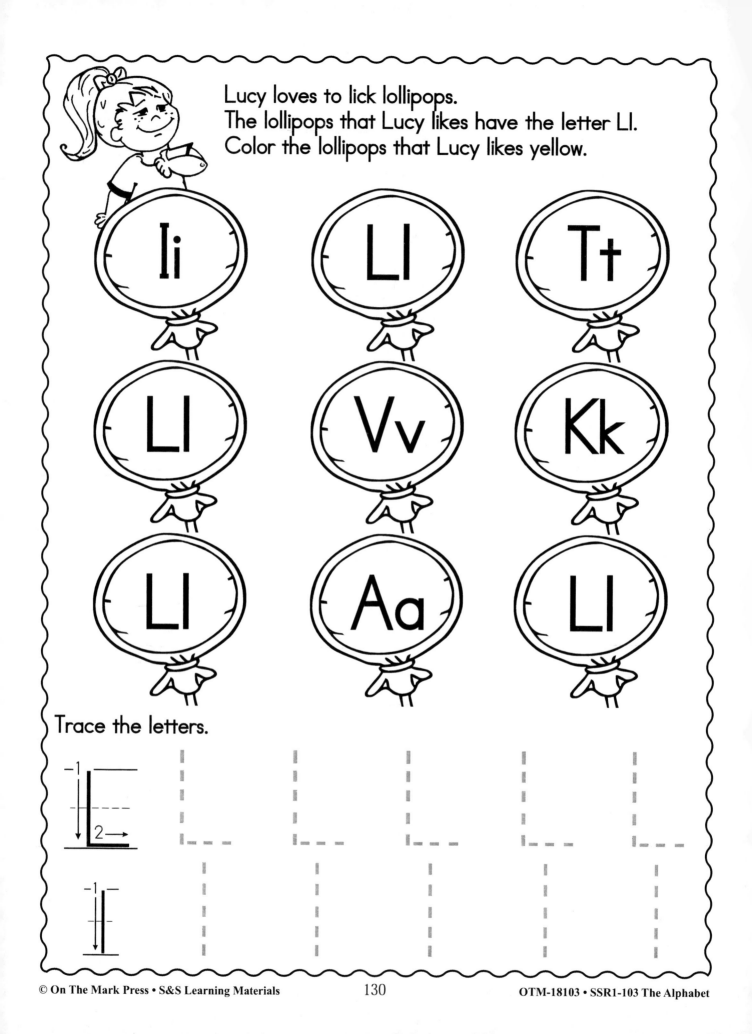

Ii   Ll   Tt

Ll   Vv   Kk

Ll   Aa   Ll

Trace the letters.

Morris Mouse loves cheese.
He only eats the cheese with the letter Mm.
Color his cheese orange.

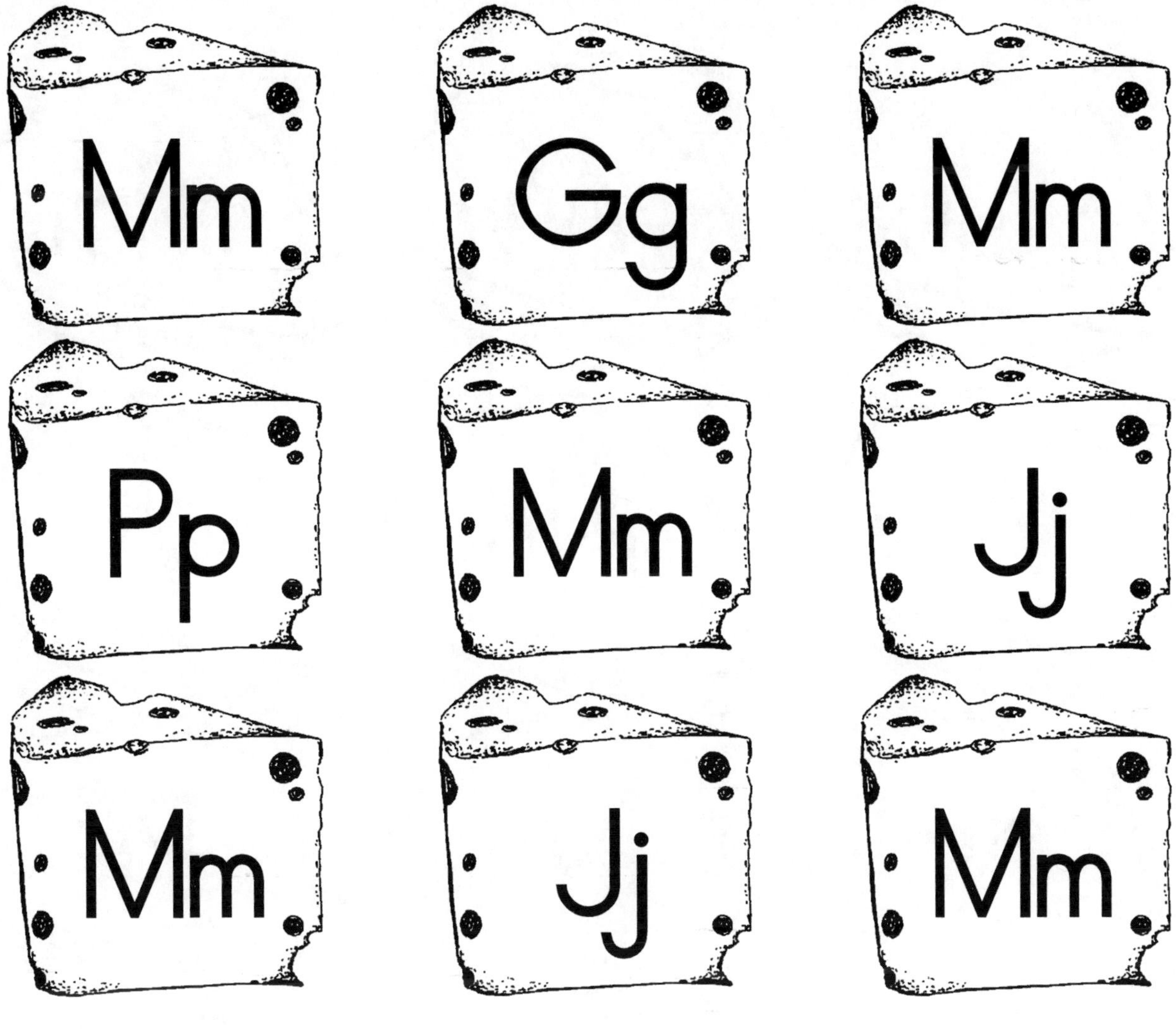

Mm   Gg   Mm

Pp   Mm   Jj

Mm   Jj   Mm

Trace the letters.

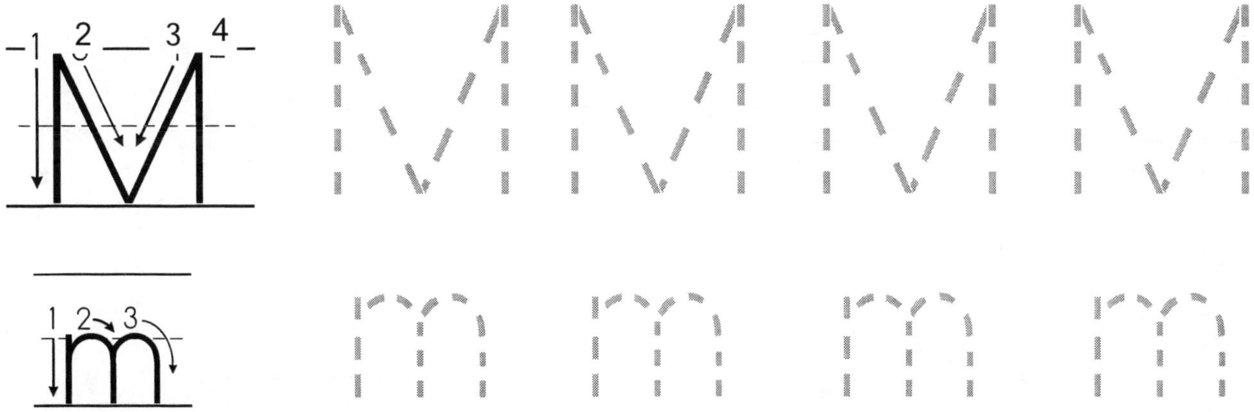

M M M M M

m m m m m

Nicky loves to eat nuts.
He eats nuts that have the letter Nn.
Color the nuts brown.

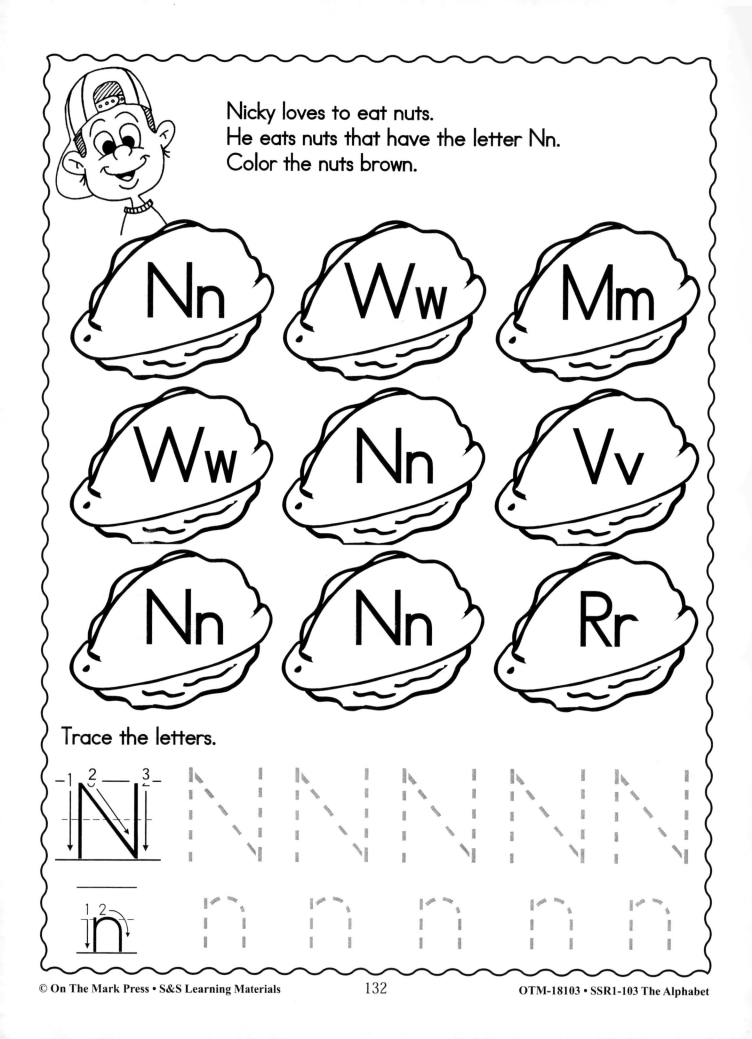

Trace the letters.

Oliver Octopus likes to chase fish.
He likes to chase fish that have the letter Oo.
Color the fish yellow that he chases.

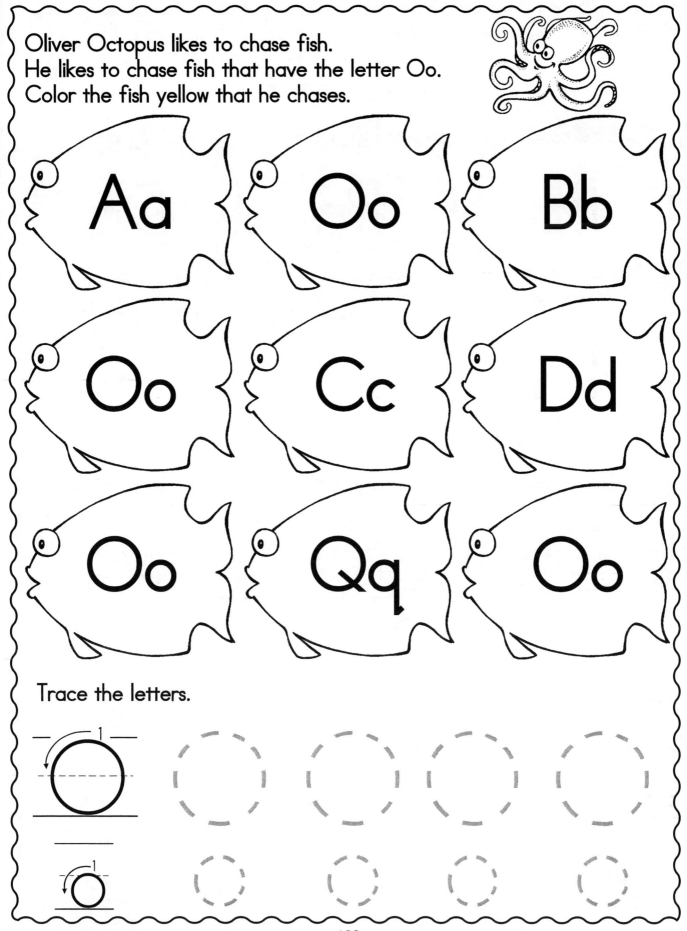

Trace the letters.

Poppy Pig loves to eat pumpkins.
She likes the ones that have Pp on them the best.
Color the pumpkins she likes the best orange.

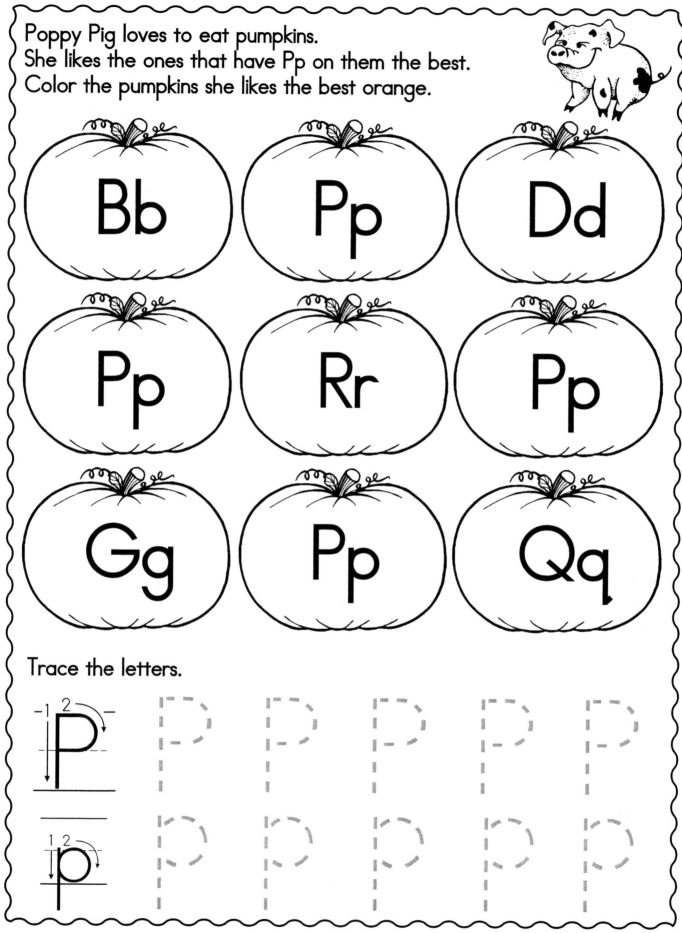

Bb Pp Dd

Pp Rr Pp

Gg Pp Qq

Trace the letters.

P P P P P P P

P P P P P P P

The Queen of Hearts is working on her quilt.
Her quilts have the letter Qq on them.
Color her quilts red.

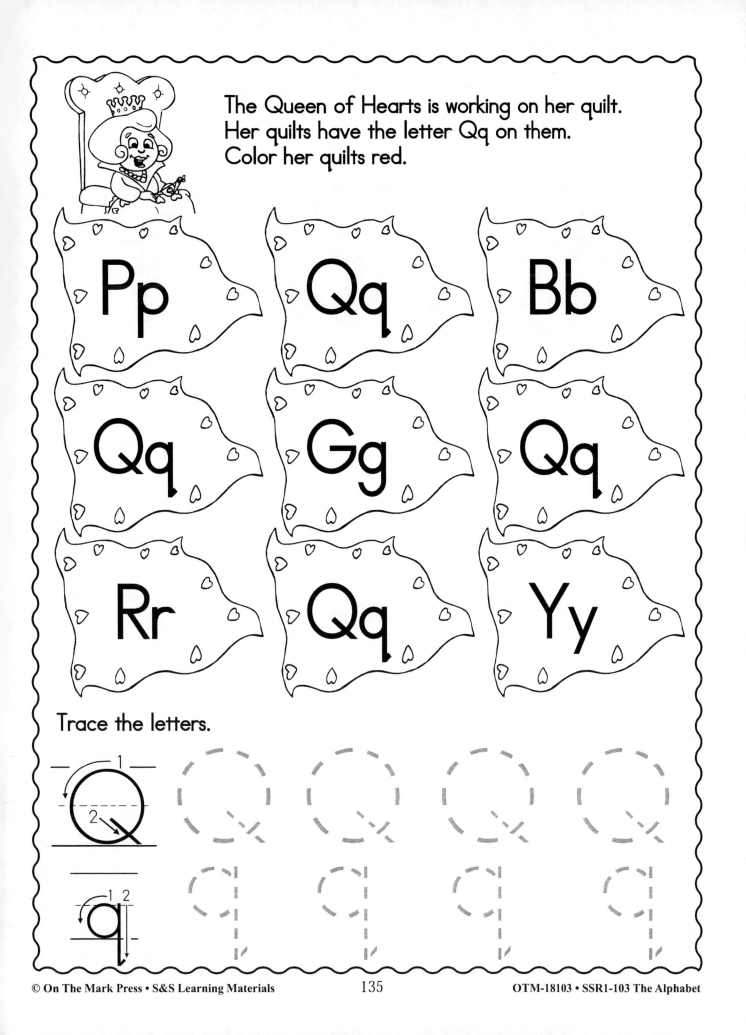

P p

Q q

B b

Q q

G g

Q q

R r

Q q

Y y

Trace the letters.

Roger Raccoon likes to climb trees.
He only climbs the trees with the letter Rr.
Color the trees that Roger climbs green.

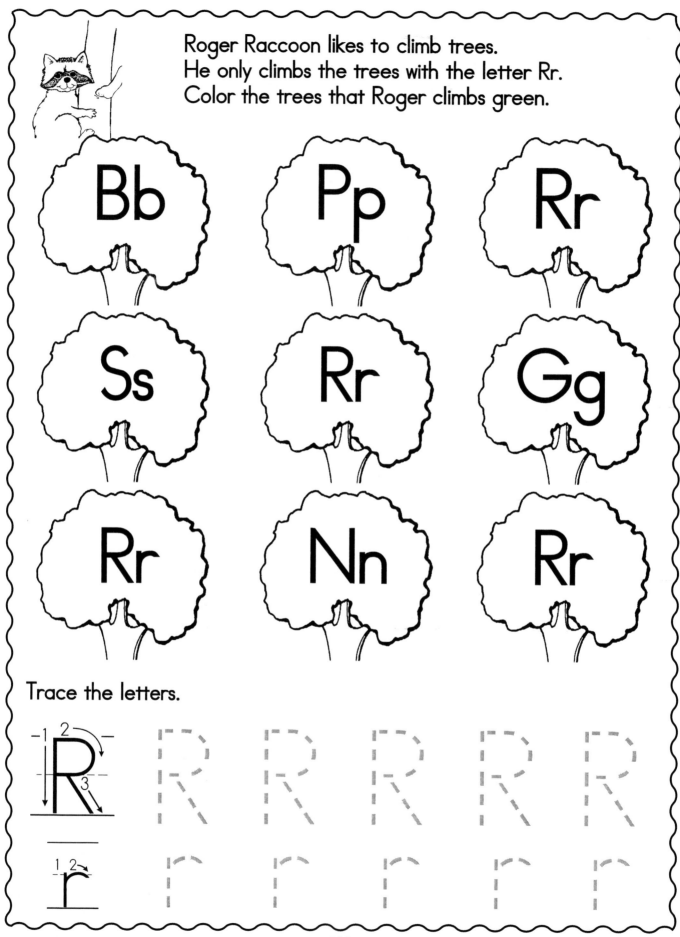

Trace the letters.

Sammy Seal likes to play with a ball.
He only plays with balls that have the letter Ss.
Color Sammy's balls green and yellow.

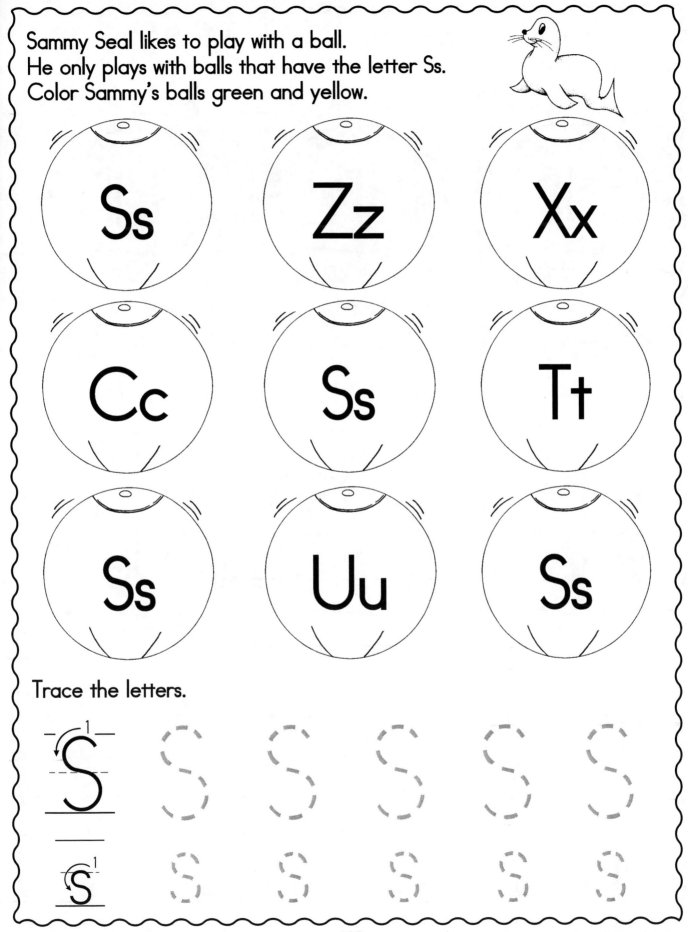

S s   Z z   X x

C c   S s   T t

S s   U u   S s

Trace the letters.

S S S S S S

s s s s s s

Timmy Turtle lives in a pond.
He likes ponds that have the letter Tt.
Color the ponds he likes blue.

Ii   Tt   Ll

Tt   Nn   Tt

Vv   Tt   Uu

Trace the letters.

Eric uses an umbrella when it rains
He likes the ones with the letter Uu.
Color the umbrellas that Eric likes yellow.

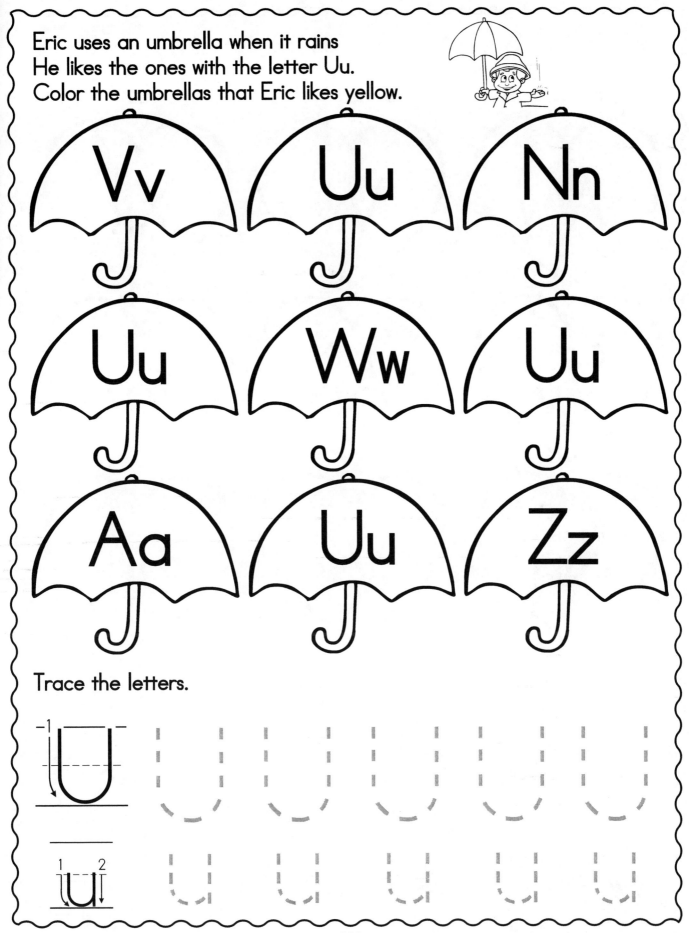

Trace the letters.

On Valentine's Day, I like to give to my friends.
I give them valentines that have a Vv.
Color the valentines that I give red.

Ww Vv Xx

Vv Aa Vv

Nn Vv Uu

Trace the letters.

V V V V V V

v v v v v v

Wilma Witch loves to make soup in her big pot.
She only makes soup in the pots that have the letter Ww.
Color those pots black.

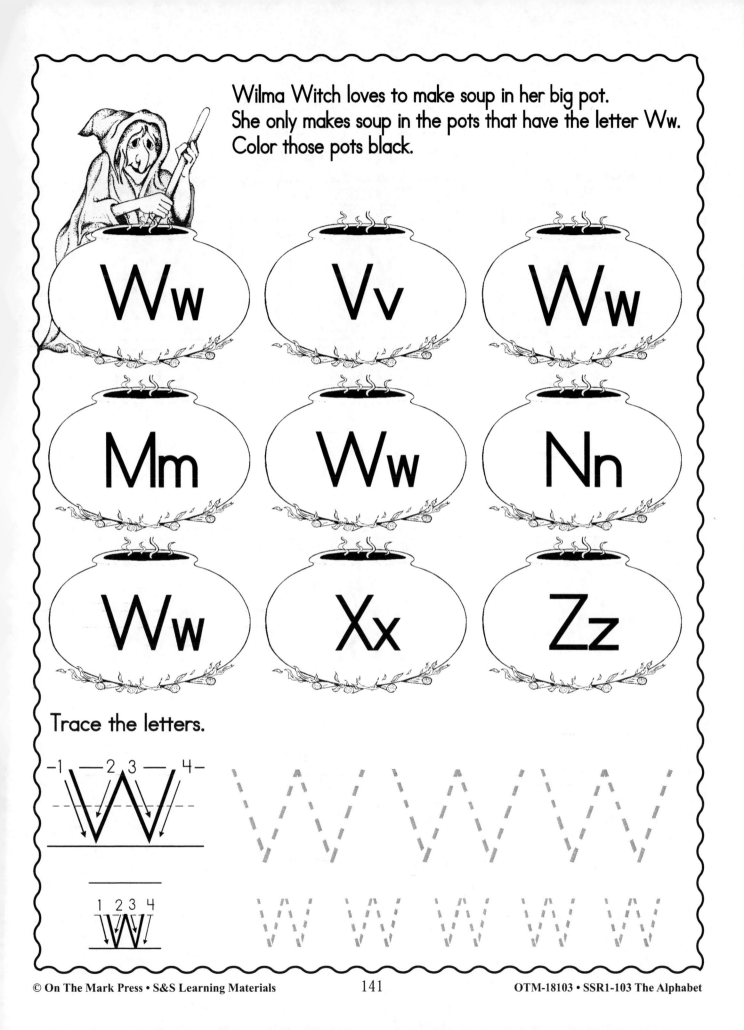

Trace the letters.

Xavier went to the hospital to have an x-ray.
He liked the ones that had an Xx on them.
Color the x-rays that Xavier liked any color.

X-RAY	X-RAY	X-RAY
Zz	Xx	Yy
Zz	Ww	Xx
Mm	Xx	Nn

Trace the letters.

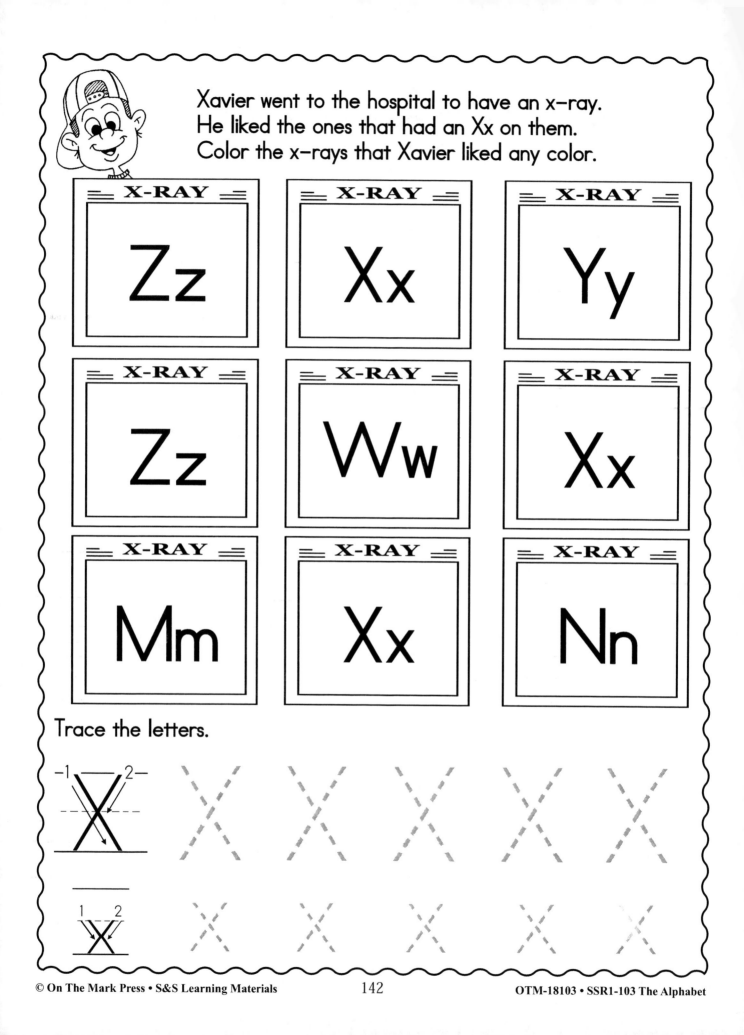

Yolanda likes to make her yoyo go up and down on its string.
Her yoyos have the letter Yy on them.
Color Yolanda's yoyos purple.

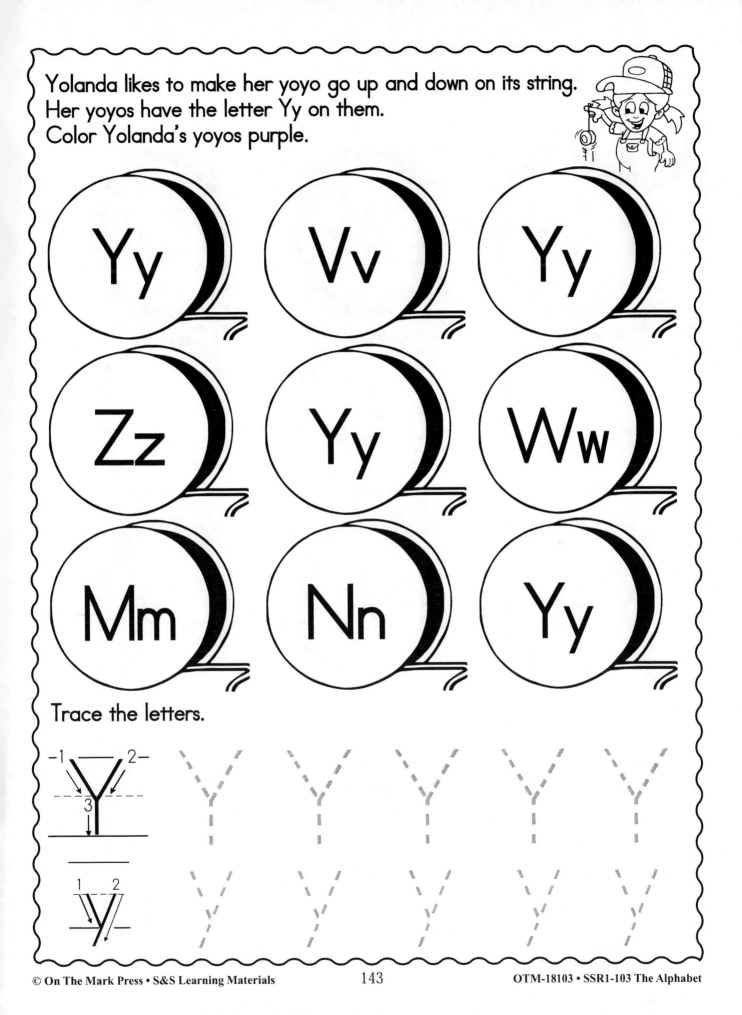

Trace the letters.

A zero is a number.
It means that you have nothing.
Color all the zeros that have the letter Zz brown.

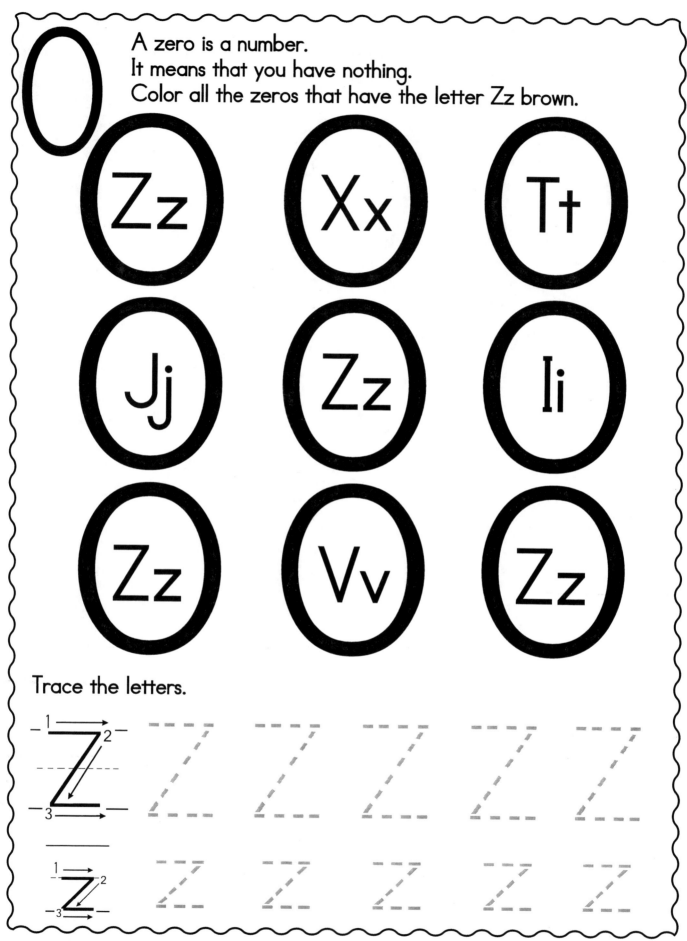

Trace the letters.